50 Japan Winter Dinner Recipes for Home

By: Kelly Johnson

Table of Contents

- Shabu-Shabu
- Sukiyaki
- Tonkotsu Ramen
- Miso Ramen
- Yudofu (Tofu Hot Pot)
- Oden
- Udon Noodle Soup
- Chanko Nabe
- Kiritanpo Nabe
- Katsu Don
- Tempura Udon
- Buta Kakuni
- Gyudon
- Nikujaga
- Tori Nabe (Chicken Hot Pot)
- Motsunabe
- Kake Udon
- Koya Dofu Stew
- Tori Dango Soup
- Salmon Nabe
- Daikon Radish Soup
- Chashu Ramen
- Tofu and Vegetable Hot Pot
- Hōba Miso Grilled Fish
- Paitan Ramen
- Chicken Karage
- Agedashi Tofu
- Katsu Curry
- Japanese Stewed Pork Belly
- Shio Ramen
- Ramen with Soft-Boiled Egg
- Teriyaki Chicken

- Chawanmushi
- Sweet Potato and Miso Stew
- Miso Soup with Seaweed
- Shrimp Tempura Udon
- Tori Soboro Don
- Beef Udon
- Tonkotsu Stew
- Okonomiyaki
- Niku Jaga
- Japanese Meatballs
- Pork and Vegetable Hot Pot
- Kinpira Gobo
- Sweet and Sour Pork
- Japanese Mushroom Soup
- Tofu and Pork Hot Pot
- Spicy Miso Ramen
- Teriyaki Beef Bowl
- Japanese Clam Soup

Shabu-Shabu

Ingredients:

- **200-300g thinly sliced beef** (sirloin or ribeye)
- **200g napa cabbage** (cut into bite-sized pieces)
- **200g mushrooms** (shiitake, enoki, or any variety you like)
- **200g tofu** (cut into cubes)
- **1-2 carrots** (sliced thinly)
- **1-2 green onions** (sliced)
- **200g udon noodles** (optional)
- **6-8 cups dashi stock** (or water with dashi powder)
- **1-2 tablespoons soy sauce**
- **1-2 tablespoons mirin** (sweet rice wine)
- **1 tablespoon sake** (optional)

For the dipping sauces:

- **Ponzu sauce** (citrus-based soy sauce)
- **Sesame dipping sauce** (or store-bought)

Instructions:

1. **Prepare the Broth:**
   - In a large pot, bring dashi stock (or water with dashi powder) to a simmer. Add soy sauce, mirin, and sake if using. Keep the broth simmering on the stove.
2. **Prepare the Ingredients:**
   - Arrange the beef slices, napa cabbage, mushrooms, tofu, carrots, and green onions on a serving platter.
3. **Cook the Ingredients:**
   - Bring the broth to a rolling boil at the table. Using chopsticks or a slotted spoon, cook the beef slices, vegetables, tofu, and mushrooms in the simmering broth until they are cooked to your liking.
4. **Serve and Enjoy:**
   - Dip the cooked ingredients into the dipping sauces of your choice. If using udon noodles, add them to the pot towards the end of cooking to soak up the flavorful broth.
5. **Finish the Broth:**
   - Once all the ingredients have been eaten, you can enjoy the remaining broth as a soup or cook the udon noodles in it if you haven't added them already.

Shabu-Shabu is all about enjoying the process of cooking and eating together, so feel free to adjust ingredients and dipping sauces to suit your taste!

Sukiyaki

Ingredients:

- **300-400g thinly sliced beef** (sirloin or ribeye)
- **200g tofu** (cut into cubes)
- **200g napa cabbage** (cut into bite-sized pieces)
- **200g mushrooms** (shiitake, enoki, or other varieties)
- **1-2 carrots** (sliced thinly)
- **1-2 green onions** (sliced)
- **100g shirataki noodles** (or udon noodles, optional)
- **1 tablespoon vegetable oil**

For the Sukiyaki Sauce (Warishita):

- **1/2 cup soy sauce**
- **1/2 cup mirin** (sweet rice wine)
- **1/4 cup sake** (optional)
- **1/4 cup sugar**

Instructions:

1. **Prepare the Sauce:**
   - In a small saucepan, combine soy sauce, mirin, sake, and sugar. Heat over medium heat until the sugar is dissolved and the sauce is well mixed. Set aside.
2. **Prepare the Ingredients:**
   - Arrange the sliced beef, tofu, vegetables, mushrooms, and shirataki noodles on a platter.
3. **Cook the Sukiyaki:**
   - Heat vegetable oil in a large skillet or hot pot over medium heat.
   - Add a few slices of beef to the pan and cook until browned. If desired, add a bit of sauce at this point to flavor the beef.
   - Once the beef is partially cooked, add some vegetables, tofu, and mushrooms to the pan.
   - Pour some of the sukiyaki sauce over the ingredients and let everything simmer until cooked. You can add more sauce as needed.
   - If using shirataki or udon noodles, add them towards the end of cooking to heat through.
4. **Serve:**
   - Serve the Sukiyaki hot from the pan. Each person can take what they like and dip it into additional sukiyaki sauce if desired.

Sukiyaki is often enjoyed as a communal meal, where everyone cooks and eats together, making it a great dish for gatherings and family dinners.

Tonkotsu Ramen

Ingredients:

For the Tonkotsu Broth:

- **2-3 lbs pork bones** (preferably neck bones or femur bones)
- **1 onion** (quartered)
- **1 head of garlic** (halved)
- **1-2 slices ginger** (smashed)
- **2-3 green onions** (cut into pieces)
- **Water** (enough to cover the bones)

For the Toppings:

- **200-300g ramen noodles** (fresh or dried)
- **2-4 slices Chashu pork** (braised pork belly)
- **1-2 soft-boiled eggs** (marinated in soy sauce, optional)
- **1 cup bamboo shoots** (menma)
- **1 cup bean sprouts**
- **1-2 green onions** (sliced thinly)
- **1 sheet nori (seaweed)** (cut into strips)
- **1-2 tablespoons sesame seeds** (optional)

For the Seasoning (Tare):

- **1/4 cup soy sauce**
- **1/4 cup mirin** (sweet rice wine)
- **1 tablespoon sake**
- **1 tablespoon miso paste** (optional, for additional depth of flavor)

Instructions:

1. **Prepare the Broth:**
   - Rinse the pork bones under cold water to remove any impurities.
   - Place the bones in a large pot and cover with water. Bring to a boil over high heat. Once boiling, discard the water and rinse the bones under cold water.
   - Refill the pot with fresh water and add the cleaned bones, onion, garlic, ginger, and green onions.
   - Bring to a boil, then reduce heat to low and simmer for 4-6 hours, occasionally skimming off any foam or fat that rises to the surface. The longer you simmer, the richer and creamier the broth will become.

- Strain the broth through a fine-mesh sieve or cheesecloth to remove the solids. Return the broth to the pot and keep warm.
2. **Prepare the Tare:**
    - In a small bowl, combine soy sauce, mirin, sake, and miso paste (if using). Stir until the miso is dissolved.
3. **Cook the Noodles:**
    - Cook the ramen noodles according to the package instructions. Drain and set aside.
4. **Assemble the Ramen:**
    - Divide the cooked noodles between serving bowls.
    - Pour a portion of the tare into each bowl over the noodles.
    - Ladle the hot tonkotsu broth over the noodles, filling the bowl.
    - Top with Chashu pork slices, soft-boiled eggs, bamboo shoots, bean sprouts, sliced green onions, and nori strips.
    - Sprinkle with sesame seeds if desired.
5. **Serve:**
    - Serve the Tonkotsu Ramen hot, and enjoy!

This recipe creates a rich, creamy ramen that's perfect for a hearty and satisfying meal. Adjust the toppings and seasoning to suit your taste!

Miso Ramen

Ingredients:

For the Miso Broth:

- **4 cups chicken or vegetable broth** (store-bought or homemade)
- **1/4 cup white miso paste** (or a mix of white and red miso for deeper flavor)
- **2 tablespoons soy sauce**
- **1 tablespoon mirin** (sweet rice wine)
- **1 tablespoon sesame oil**
- **1-2 cloves garlic** (minced)
- **1 tablespoon ginger** (minced)

For the Ramen:

- **200-300g ramen noodles** (fresh or dried)
- **1 cup corn kernels** (optional)
- **1 cup bamboo shoots** (menma)
- **1-2 cups spinach** (or bok choy)
- **2-4 slices Chashu pork** (braised pork belly) or grilled chicken
- **2-4 soft-boiled eggs** (marinated in soy sauce, optional)
- **1-2 green onions** (sliced thinly)
- **1 sheet nori (seaweed)** (cut into strips)
- **1 tablespoon sesame seeds** (optional)
- **Bean sprouts** (optional)

Instructions:

1. **Prepare the Miso Broth:**
    - Heat sesame oil in a large pot over medium heat. Add minced garlic and ginger and sauté until fragrant, about 1 minute.
    - Add the chicken or vegetable broth and bring to a simmer.
    - In a small bowl, combine miso paste with a ladleful of hot broth, stirring until smooth. Add this mixture back into the pot.
    - Stir in soy sauce and mirin. Simmer the broth for 5-10 minutes to let the flavors meld. Adjust seasoning to taste if needed. Keep warm.
2. **Prepare the Toppings:**
    - **Cook the Noodles:** Cook the ramen noodles according to the package instructions. Drain and set aside.
    - **Prepare the Corn and Spinach:** If using corn, you can either use canned or frozen corn. For spinach or bok choy, blanch briefly in boiling water or sauté until wilted.

3. **Assemble the Ramen:**
    - Divide the cooked noodles between serving bowls.
    - Pour the hot miso broth over the noodles.
    - Top with Chashu pork slices (or grilled chicken), bamboo shoots, spinach, corn, and any other desired toppings.
    - Add soft-boiled eggs, sliced green onions, nori strips, and sesame seeds if using.
    - Garnish with additional bean sprouts if desired.
4. **Serve:**
    - Serve the Miso Ramen hot and enjoy!

This recipe offers a rich and comforting bowl of Miso Ramen, with a savory broth balanced by the umami of miso and the freshness of the toppings. Adjust the toppings and ingredients based on your preferences and availability!

Yudofu (Tofu Hot Pot)

Ingredients:

For the Hot Pot:

- **1 block firm tofu** (cut into cubes)
- **4-6 cups dashi broth** (or water with dashi powder)
- **1-2 cups napa cabbage** (cut into bite-sized pieces)
- **1-2 carrots** (sliced thinly)
- **1 cup mushrooms** (shiitake, enoki, or other varieties)
- **1-2 green onions** (sliced)
- **1 tablespoon soy sauce**
- **1 tablespoon mirin** (sweet rice wine)

For the Dipping Sauces:

- **Ponzu sauce** (citrus-based soy sauce)
- **Sesame dipping sauce** (store-bought or homemade)

Optional Garnishes:

- **Shredded daikon radish**
- **Chopped fresh herbs** (like cilantro or green onions)
- **Grated yuzu or lemon zest**

Instructions:

1. **Prepare the Broth:**
    - In a large pot, bring dashi broth (or water with dashi powder) to a gentle simmer. Add soy sauce and mirin. Adjust seasoning to taste. Keep the broth warm on the stove.
2. **Prepare the Ingredients:**
    - Arrange the tofu cubes, napa cabbage, carrots, mushrooms, and green onions on a serving platter.
3. **Cook the Ingredients:**
    - Bring the broth to a gentle simmer at the table. Using chopsticks or a slotted spoon, cook the tofu cubes, vegetables, and mushrooms in the simmering broth until they are cooked through and tender. The tofu should be heated thoroughly, and the vegetables should be slightly softened but still crisp.
4. **Serve:**
    - Transfer cooked ingredients to individual bowls.

- Serve with dipping sauces on the side. Each person can dip the cooked tofu and vegetables into the sauces of their choice.
5. **Optional:**
    - Garnish with shredded daikon radish, fresh herbs, or grated yuzu/lemon zest for extra flavor.

Yudofu is a comforting and healthy dish, perfect for cold weather. It's also versatile, so feel free to adjust the ingredients and dipping sauces to suit your taste.

Oden

Ingredients:

For the Broth:

- **6-8 cups dashi broth** (homemade or store-bought, or water with dashi powder)
- **1/4 cup soy sauce**
- **1/4 cup mirin** (sweet rice wine)
- **2 tablespoons sake** (optional)
- **1-2 tablespoons sugar** (adjust to taste)

For the Oden Ingredients:

- **1 daikon radish** (peeled and cut into thick rounds)
- **4-6 eggs** (hard-boiled and peeled)
- **1 block tofu** (cut into cubes, or use fried tofu puffs)
- **1 package konnyaku** (sliced or cut into pieces, optional)
- **4-6 fish cakes** (such as chikuwa, hanpen, or oden-nyu)
- **1-2 pieces of kombu** (dried kelp, optional)
- **1-2 carrots** (sliced thickly, optional)
- **Shirataki noodles** (optional)

For Serving:

- **Mustard** (karashi) for dipping
- **Ponzu sauce** or **soy sauce** (for extra seasoning if desired)

Instructions:

1. **Prepare the Broth:**
    - In a large pot, combine dashi broth, soy sauce, mirin, sake (if using), and sugar. Stir well and bring to a simmer.
2. **Prepare the Ingredients:**
    - **Daikon Radish:** Peel and cut into thick rounds. Parboil in a separate pot for 10 minutes to remove bitterness and then add to the main pot.
    - **Eggs:** Hard-boil eggs, peel, and set aside.
    - **Tofu:** Cut into cubes or use pre-fried tofu puffs.
    - **Konnyaku:** Slice or cut into pieces, if using.
    - **Fish Cakes:** Prepare by cutting into bite-sized pieces if necessary.
3. **Cook the Oden:**
    - Add the prepared daikon radish, tofu, konnyaku, fish cakes, carrots (if using), and kombu (if using) to the simmering broth.

- Simmer for 30-45 minutes, or until the daikon radish and other ingredients are tender and have absorbed the flavors of the broth.
 - Add the hard-boiled eggs during the last 10-15 minutes of cooking to allow them to absorb some of the flavors.
4. **Serve:**
 - Ladle the Oden into bowls, making sure to include a variety of ingredients in each serving.
 - Serve hot with mustard and additional dipping sauces on the side if desired.
5. **Optional:**
 - Garnish with chopped green onions or additional kombu if desired.

Oden is meant to be a comforting and hearty dish, ideal for sharing with family and friends. Feel free to customize it with your favorite ingredients and adjust the seasoning to your taste!

Udon Noodle Soup

Ingredients:

For the Broth:

- **4 cups dashi broth** (or chicken/vegetable broth with dashi powder)
- **1/4 cup soy sauce**
- **2 tablespoons mirin** (sweet rice wine)
- **1 tablespoon sake** (optional)
- **1-2 tablespoons sugar** (adjust to taste)

For the Soup:

- **200-300g fresh or dried udon noodles**
- **1 cup mushrooms** (shiitake, enoki, or other varieties, sliced)
- **1 cup spinach** (or bok choy)
- **1-2 green onions** (sliced)
- **1/2 cup bamboo shoots** (menma, optional)
- **1 block tofu** (cubed or sliced, optional)
- **2-4 soft-boiled eggs** (optional)
- **2-4 slices Chashu pork** (or grilled chicken, optional)
- **1 sheet nori (seaweed)** (cut into strips, optional)

For Garnish:

- **Sesame seeds**
- **Chili oil** or **shichimi togarashi** (Japanese seven-spice blend)
- **Fresh herbs** (like cilantro or green onions)

Instructions:

1. **Prepare the Broth:**
    - In a large pot, combine dashi broth (or chicken/vegetable broth with dashi powder), soy sauce, mirin, and sake (if using). Stir well and bring to a simmer.
    - Adjust the seasoning with sugar if needed. Keep the broth warm on the stove.
2. **Prepare the Noodles:**
    - Cook the udon noodles according to the package instructions. Drain and rinse under cold water to prevent sticking. Set aside.
3. **Prepare the Soup Ingredients:**
    - **Mushrooms:** Slice and prepare as needed.
    - **Spinach:** Blanch briefly in boiling water or sauté until wilted.
    - **Tofu:** Cut into cubes or slices, if using.

- **Bamboo Shoots:** Rinse and set aside, if using.

4. **Assemble the Soup:**
   - Add the mushrooms, tofu, and bamboo shoots (if using) to the simmering broth. Cook for 5-7 minutes until the vegetables are tender.
   - Add the cooked udon noodles and spinach to the pot. Heat through for a couple of minutes.

5. **Serve:**
   - Divide the noodles and soup ingredients between serving bowls.
   - Ladle the hot broth over the noodles and ingredients.
   - Top with soft-boiled eggs, Chashu pork (or grilled chicken), green onions, and nori strips if desired.

6. **Garnish:**
   - Sprinkle with sesame seeds, chili oil, or shichimi togarashi for added flavor and heat.
   - Garnish with fresh herbs if using.

Tips:

- **Broth:** The dashi broth can be homemade or store-bought. If using store-bought broth, adjust the seasoning as needed.
- **Noodles:** Fresh udon noodles are ideal, but dried udon noodles work well too. Be sure to cook them according to the package instructions.
- **Toppings:** Feel free to customize the toppings based on your preference or availability.

Enjoy your warm, hearty bowl of Udon Noodle Soup!

Chanko Nabe

Ingredients:

For the Broth:

- **6-8 cups dashi broth** (or chicken/vegetable broth with dashi powder)
- **1/4 cup soy sauce**
- **1/4 cup mirin** (sweet rice wine)
- **2 tablespoons sake** (optional)
- **1-2 tablespoons miso paste** (optional, for additional depth of flavor)

For the Hot Pot:

- **200-300g chicken thighs** (cut into bite-sized pieces, boneless)
- **200g tofu** (cut into cubes)
- **1-2 carrots** (sliced thinly or cut into rounds)
- **1 cup mushrooms** (shiitake, enoki, or other varieties)
- **1 cup napa cabbage** (cut into bite-sized pieces)
- **1 cup bok choy** (or spinach)
- **1-2 green onions** (sliced)
- **1-2 cups daikon radish** (peeled and sliced into rounds)
- **1 package konnyaku** (sliced or cut into pieces, optional)
- **1-2 sheets kombu** (dried kelp, optional)
- **200-300g udon noodles** (or other noodles like soba or ramen, optional)
- **1 cup fish cakes** (such as chikuwa or hanpen, optional)

For Serving:

- **Ponzu sauce** (citrus-based soy sauce)
- **Sesame dipping sauce** (or other dipping sauces of your choice)
- **Shichimi togarashi** (Japanese seven-spice blend, optional)
- **Chopped fresh herbs** (like green onions or cilantro, optional)

Instructions:

1. **Prepare the Broth:**
    - In a large pot, combine dashi broth (or chicken/vegetable broth with dashi powder), soy sauce, mirin, and sake (if using). Stir well and bring to a simmer. Add miso paste if using, and dissolve completely. Keep warm.
2. **Prepare the Ingredients:**
    - Arrange the chicken pieces, tofu, carrots, mushrooms, napa cabbage, bok choy, daikon radish, konnyaku (if using), and kombu (if using) on a platter.

3. **Cook the Hot Pot:**
    - Bring the broth to a gentle simmer at the table. Add the chicken pieces first and cook until fully cooked through, about 5-7 minutes.
    - Add the vegetables, tofu, and konnyaku (if using) to the pot. Simmer until the vegetables are tender, about 10-15 minutes.
    - Add the fish cakes (if using) and cook for an additional 2-3 minutes.
    - If using noodles, cook them separately according to package instructions, then add them to the pot towards the end of cooking, just to heat through.
4. **Serve:**
    - Ladle the hot pot ingredients and broth into individual bowls.
    - Serve with dipping sauces on the side. Each person can dip their ingredients into ponzu sauce or sesame sauce for added flavor.
5. **Garnish:**
    - Garnish with shichimi togarashi and fresh herbs if desired.

Tips:

- **Broth:** Adjust the seasoning of the broth according to your taste. The broth can be made richer by simmering longer or adding more ingredients.
- **Ingredients:** Feel free to customize the ingredients based on your preferences or what you have on hand. Other common additions include seafood, different types of meat, or additional vegetables.

Chanko Nabe is a versatile and satisfying dish perfect for cold weather or a hearty meal with family and friends. Enjoy your warm and comforting hot pot!

Kiritanpo Nabe

Ingredients:

For the Broth:

- **6-8 cups dashi broth** (or chicken/vegetable broth with dashi powder)
- **1/4 cup soy sauce**
- **2 tablespoons mirin** (sweet rice wine)
- **1 tablespoon sake** (optional)
- **1-2 tablespoons miso paste** (optional, for extra depth)

For the Hot Pot:

- **200-300g chicken thighs** (boneless, cut into bite-sized pieces)
- **2-4 kiritanpo sticks** (or use homemade or store-bought rice cakes, if kiritanpo is not available)
- **1 cup mushrooms** (shiitake, enoki, or other varieties, sliced)
- **1-2 carrots** (sliced thinly or cut into rounds)
- **1 cup napa cabbage** (cut into bite-sized pieces)
- **1 cup bamboo shoots** (menma, optional)
- **1 cup tofu** (cut into cubes, optional)
- **1-2 green onions** (sliced)
- **1-2 cups spinach** (or bok choy)

For Serving:

- **Ponzu sauce** (citrus-based soy sauce)
- **Sesame dipping sauce** (or other dipping sauces of your choice)
- **Shichimi togarashi** (Japanese seven-spice blend, optional)
- **Chopped fresh herbs** (like green onions or cilantro, optional)

Instructions:

1. **Prepare the Broth:**
    - In a large pot, combine dashi broth (or chicken/vegetable broth with dashi powder), soy sauce, mirin, and sake (if using). Stir well and bring to a simmer. Add miso paste if desired and stir until dissolved. Keep warm.
2. **Prepare the Kiritanpo:**
    - If using store-bought kiritanpo, they are usually pre-grilled. If you're making them from scratch, mold cooked rice onto skewers and grill or toast them until slightly crispy on the outside.
3. **Prepare the Ingredients:**

- Arrange the chicken pieces, mushrooms, carrots, napa cabbage, bamboo shoots, tofu, and green onions on a platter.

4. **Cook the Hot Pot:**
   - Bring the broth to a gentle simmer at the table. Add the chicken pieces first and cook until fully cooked, about 5-7 minutes.
   - Add the vegetables, tofu, and bamboo shoots (if using). Simmer until the vegetables are tender, about 10-15 minutes.
   - Add the kiritanpo sticks and cook until heated through and infused with the flavors of the broth, about 5-7 minutes.
   - Add spinach (or bok choy) in the last few minutes of cooking.
5. **Serve:**
   - Ladle the hot pot ingredients and broth into individual bowls.
   - Serve with dipping sauces on the side. Each person can dip their ingredients into ponzu sauce or sesame sauce.
6. **Garnish:**
   - Garnish with shichimi togarashi and fresh herbs if desired.

Tips:

- **Broth:** Adjust the seasoning of the broth according to your taste. You can add more soy sauce or miso if you prefer a richer flavor.
- **Kiritanpo:** If you can't find kiritanpo, you can substitute with regular rice cakes or cooked rice, though the texture will be slightly different.

Kiritanpo Nabe is a flavorful and satisfying hot pot that's perfect for family meals or gatherings. Enjoy the hearty combination of grilled rice and savory broth!

Katsu Don

Ingredients:

For the Tonkatsu:

- **2 boneless pork chops** (or pork loin, about 1/2 inch thick)
- **Salt and pepper** (to taste)
- **1/2 cup all-purpose flour**
- **1 egg** (beaten)
- **1 cup panko breadcrumbs** (Japanese breadcrumbs)
- **Vegetable oil** (for frying)

For the Katsu Don Sauce:

- **1/2 cup dashi broth** (or chicken/vegetable broth with dashi powder)
- **1/4 cup soy sauce**
- **1/4 cup mirin** (sweet rice wine)
- **2 tablespoons sugar**

For the Katsu Don Bowl:

- **1 onion** (sliced thinly)
- **2-3 eggs** (beaten)
- **2 cups cooked white rice** (warm)
- **2 green onions** (sliced, for garnish)
- **1 tablespoon chopped parsley or shiso leaves** (optional, for garnish)

Instructions:

1. **Prepare the Tonkatsu:**
   - Season the pork chops with salt and pepper.
   - Dredge each pork chop in flour, shaking off excess.
   - Dip in beaten egg, allowing excess to drip off.
   - Coat with panko breadcrumbs, pressing gently to adhere.
   - Heat vegetable oil in a large skillet over medium-high heat. Fry the pork chops until golden brown and cooked through, about 4-5 minutes per side. Drain on paper towels and let cool slightly.
   - Slice the cooked pork into strips.
2. **Prepare the Katsu Don Sauce:**
   - In a small saucepan, combine dashi broth, soy sauce, mirin, and sugar. Bring to a simmer over medium heat, stirring until the sugar is dissolved. Set aside.
3. **Assemble the Katsu Don:**

- In a large skillet or shallow pan, heat a small amount of oil over medium heat. Add the sliced onion and cook until softened.
- Pour the Katsu Don sauce over the onions and bring to a simmer.
- Arrange the sliced pork on top of the onions in the skillet. Pour the beaten eggs over the pork and onions.
- Cover and cook for 2-3 minutes, or until the eggs are set but still slightly soft.

4. **Serve:**
   - Place a portion of warm cooked rice in each serving bowl.
   - Spoon the pork and onion mixture with the sauce over the rice.
   - Garnish with sliced green onions and chopped parsley or shiso leaves if desired.

5. **Optional:**
   - Serve with additional pickled vegetables or a side salad if desired.

Tips:

- **Tonkatsu:** For a crispy tonkatsu, ensure the oil is hot enough before frying and avoid overcrowding the pan.
- **Eggs:** The eggs should be slightly runny when cooked for the best texture, but you can cook them longer if you prefer them firmer.

Katsu Don is a hearty and satisfying dish, perfect for a comforting meal. Enjoy the delicious combination of crispy pork, savory sauce, and tender eggs over rice!

Tempura Udon

Ingredients:

For the Broth:

- **4 cups dashi broth** (or chicken/vegetable broth with dashi powder)
- **1/4 cup soy sauce**
- **2 tablespoons mirin** (sweet rice wine)
- **1 tablespoon sake** (optional)
- **1 tablespoon sugar** (adjust to taste)

For the Tempura:

- **1/2 cup all-purpose flour**
- **1/4 cup cornstarch**
- **1/4 teaspoon baking powder**
- **1/2 cup cold water** (ice-cold is best)
- **1 egg** (lightly beaten)
- **Vegetable oil** (for frying)

For Tempura Ingredients:

- **1 cup shrimp** (peeled and deveined)
- **1 cup assorted vegetables** (such as sweet potatoes, zucchini, or mushrooms, sliced)

For the Udon:

- **200-300g udon noodles** (fresh or dried)
- **1 cup green onions** (sliced thinly)
- **1 sheet nori (seaweed)** (cut into strips, optional)
- **1 tablespoon sesame seeds** (optional)

Instructions:

1. **Prepare the Broth:**
   - In a large pot, combine dashi broth (or chicken/vegetable broth with dashi powder), soy sauce, mirin, and sake (if using). Stir well and bring to a simmer. Adjust the seasoning with sugar if needed. Keep warm.
2. **Prepare the Tempura:**
   - **Make the Tempura Batter:** In a mixing bowl, whisk together flour, cornstarch, and baking powder. Gradually add cold water and beaten egg, stirring gently until just combined. The batter should be lumpy.

- **Heat the Oil:** In a deep skillet or pot, heat about 2 inches of vegetable oil to 350°F (175°C). Use a thermometer to ensure the right temperature.
- **Fry the Tempura:** Dip shrimp and vegetable slices into the tempura batter, allowing excess to drip off. Fry in batches until golden brown and crispy, about 2-3 minutes per batch. Drain on paper towels.
3. **Prepare the Udon Noodles:**
    - Cook the udon noodles according to the package instructions. Drain and set aside.
4. **Assemble the Tempura Udon:**
    - Divide the cooked udon noodles between serving bowls.
    - Ladle the hot broth over the noodles.
    - Top with crispy tempura, sliced green onions, and nori strips if using.
    - Sprinkle with sesame seeds if desired.
5. **Serve:**
    - Serve the Tempura Udon hot, and enjoy!

Tips:

- **Tempura Batter:** For the best texture, avoid overmixing the batter. Lumpy batter will result in a crispier coating.
- **Oil Temperature:** Maintain the oil temperature between 340-360°F (170-180°C) for crispy tempura. Too hot or too cold oil can affect the texture.
- **Noodles:** Fresh udon noodles provide the best texture, but dried udon noodles are a good alternative if fresh ones aren't available.

Tempura Udon is a hearty and satisfying meal, combining the rich umami of the broth with the light, crisp texture of tempura. Enjoy this comforting Japanese classic!

Buta Kakuni

Ingredients:

For the Buta Kakuni:

- **1 lb (450g) pork belly** (cut into 1-inch cubes)
- **1 tablespoon vegetable oil**
- **1-inch piece of ginger** (sliced thinly)
- **2-3 cloves garlic** (sliced thinly)
- **1/2 cup soy sauce**
- **1/4 cup mirin** (sweet rice wine)
- **1/4 cup sake** (Japanese rice wine, optional)
- **1/4 cup sugar**
- **2-3 scallions** (cut into 2-inch pieces)
- **1 star anise** (optional, for additional depth of flavor)
- **1-2 sheets kombu (dried kelp)** (optional, for additional umami)

For Garnish:

- **Chopped green onions**
- **Shredded daikon radish** (optional)
- **Pickled vegetables** (optional)

Instructions:

1. **Prepare the Pork Belly:**
   - In a large pot or Dutch oven, heat vegetable oil over medium-high heat. Add the pork belly cubes and sear on all sides until browned, about 5-7 minutes. Remove the pork belly from the pot and set aside.
2. **Prepare the Aromatics:**
   - In the same pot, add the sliced ginger and garlic. Sauté for about 1 minute until fragrant.
3. **Deglaze and Braise:**
   - Return the pork belly to the pot. Add soy sauce, mirin, sake (if using), and sugar. Stir to combine.
   - Add scallions, star anise (if using), and kombu (if using) to the pot.
   - Pour in enough water to just cover the pork belly. Bring to a boil.
4. **Simmer:**
   - Once boiling, reduce heat to low, cover, and simmer for 1.5 to 2 hours, or until the pork belly is tender and the sauce has thickened. Stir occasionally and skim off any impurities that rise to the surface.
5. **Finish and Serve:**

- Once the pork belly is tender and the sauce has thickened to a glossy consistency, remove from heat.
- Discard the kombu and star anise if used.
6. **Garnish and Serve:**
    - Serve the Buta Kakuni over steamed rice or alongside vegetables.
    - Garnish with chopped green onions, shredded daikon radish, and pickled vegetables if desired.

Tips:

- **Pork Belly:** For the best results, use pork belly with a good balance of meat and fat.
- **Skimming:** Skim off any impurities or excess fat from the surface of the broth during cooking for a clearer, less greasy sauce.
- **Make Ahead:** Buta Kakuni tastes even better the next day as the flavors continue to develop. It can be made ahead and stored in the refrigerator for up to 3 days.

Buta Kakuni is a rich and flavorful dish perfect for a comforting meal. Enjoy the tender, savory pork belly with its sweet and salty glaze!

Gyudon

Ingredients:

For the Beef Mixture:

- **1 lb (450g) beef sirloin** (or ribeye, thinly sliced against the grain)
- **1 large onion** (sliced thinly)
- **1 tablespoon vegetable oil**
- **1/2 cup soy sauce**
- **1/4 cup mirin** (sweet rice wine)
- **1/4 cup sake** (Japanese rice wine, optional)
- **2 tablespoons sugar**
- **1 cup dashi broth** (or water with dashi powder)
- **1 tablespoon ginger** (grated or minced)
- **2-3 green onions** (sliced, for garnish)
- **1 tablespoon sesame seeds** (optional, for garnish)

For Serving:

- **4 cups steamed white rice**
- **Pickled ginger** (beni shoga, optional, for garnish)
- **Shredded nori (seaweed)** (optional, for garnish)

Instructions:

1. **Prepare the Beef Mixture:**
   - Heat vegetable oil in a large skillet or frying pan over medium-high heat.
   - Add the sliced onions and cook until softened and slightly caramelized, about 5 minutes.
   - Add the thinly sliced beef to the pan and cook until browned, about 3-4 minutes.
2. **Make the Sauce:**
   - In a small bowl, mix together soy sauce, mirin, sake (if using), sugar, and dashi broth.
   - Pour the sauce mixture over the beef and onions in the pan. Stir well to combine.
   - Add the grated ginger to the pan and stir.
3. **Simmer:**
   - Bring the mixture to a simmer and cook for 5-7 minutes, or until the sauce has reduced slightly and the beef is tender.
4. **Serve:**
   - Divide steamed rice among serving bowls.
   - Spoon the beef and onion mixture over the rice.

- Garnish with sliced green onions, sesame seeds, pickled ginger, and shredded nori if using.

Tips:

- **Beef:** Thinly sliced beef works best for Gyudon. If you can't find pre-sliced beef, freeze the beef for about 30 minutes to make it easier to slice thinly.
- **Sauce:** Adjust the sweetness or saltiness of the sauce by adding more sugar or soy sauce according to your taste.
- **Rice:** Ensure the rice is hot and fluffy to complement the flavorful beef topping.

Gyudon is a quick and delicious meal that's perfect for busy weeknights or a comforting lunch. Enjoy the rich flavors and tender beef over a bed of warm rice!

Nikujaga

Ingredients:

For the Nikujaga:

- **1/2 lb (225g) beef sirloin or ribeye** (sliced thinly)
- **3-4 medium potatoes** (peeled and cut into bite-sized chunks)
- **1 large onion** (sliced thinly)
- **1-2 carrots** (peeled and sliced into rounds, optional)
- **2 tablespoons vegetable oil**

For the Sauce:

- **1/4 cup soy sauce**
- **1/4 cup mirin** (sweet rice wine)
- **2 tablespoons sugar**
- **1/4 cup sake** (Japanese rice wine, optional)
- **1 cup dashi broth** (or water with dashi powder)

For Garnish:

- **Chopped green onions** (optional)
- **Shredded nori (seaweed)** (optional)

Instructions:

1. **Prepare the Ingredients:**
    - Peel and cut the potatoes into bite-sized chunks. If using carrots, slice them into rounds.
    - Slice the onion thinly and the beef into thin strips.
2. **Cook the Beef and Onions:**
    - Heat vegetable oil in a large pot or Dutch oven over medium-high heat.
    - Add the sliced onions and cook until they become translucent and slightly caramelized, about 5 minutes.
    - Add the sliced beef to the pot and cook until it is browned, about 3-4 minutes.
3. **Add Vegetables:**
    - Add the potatoes and carrots (if using) to the pot. Stir to combine with the beef and onions.
4. **Add the Sauce Ingredients:**
    - In a small bowl, mix together soy sauce, mirin, sugar, sake (if using), and dashi broth.
    - Pour the sauce mixture over the beef and vegetables in the pot. Stir well.

5. **Simmer:**
    - Bring the mixture to a boil, then reduce heat to low.
    - Cover the pot and simmer for 20-30 minutes, or until the potatoes and carrots are tender and the sauce has thickened. Stir occasionally and adjust seasoning if needed.
6. **Serve:**
    - Serve Nikujaga hot, directly from the pot or divided into serving bowls.
    - Garnish with chopped green onions or shredded nori if desired.

Tips:

- **Potatoes:** Use starchy potatoes like Russet or Idaho potatoes for the best texture. They hold their shape well and absorb the flavors of the sauce.
- **Beef:** Thinly sliced beef is ideal for Nikujaga, as it cooks quickly and infuses the dish with flavor.
- **Sauce:** Adjust the sweetness or saltiness of the sauce by modifying the amount of sugar or soy sauce according to your taste.

Nikujaga is a comforting and flavorful dish that pairs well with a side of steamed rice. Enjoy this classic Japanese meal that brings warmth and satisfaction to the table!

Tori Nabe (Chicken Hot Pot)

Ingredients:

For the Broth:

- **4 cups chicken broth** (or dashi broth for added umami)
- **1/4 cup soy sauce**
- **2 tablespoons mirin** (sweet rice wine)
- **2 tablespoons sake** (Japanese rice wine, optional)
- **1 tablespoon sugar** (adjust to taste)

For the Hot Pot:

- **1 lb (450g) chicken thighs** (boneless, cut into bite-sized pieces)
- **1 cup mushrooms** (shiitake, enoki, or other varieties)
- **1-2 carrots** (peeled and sliced into rounds)
- **1 cup napa cabbage** (cut into bite-sized pieces)
- **1 cup bok choy** (or spinach)
- **1 block tofu** (cut into cubes, optional)
- **1-2 green onions** (sliced)
- **1-2 sheets kombu (dried kelp)** (optional, for extra umami)
- **1 cup udon noodles** (or soba/ramen, optional)

For Garnish:

- **Chopped green onions**
- **Shichimi togarashi** (Japanese seven-spice blend, optional)
- **Sesame seeds** (optional)
- **Fresh herbs** (like cilantro or parsley, optional)

Instructions:

1. **Prepare the Broth:**
   - In a large pot, combine chicken broth, soy sauce, mirin, sake (if using), and sugar. Stir well and bring to a simmer. Adjust the seasoning to taste and keep warm.
2. **Prepare the Ingredients:**
   - Cut chicken thighs into bite-sized pieces.
   - Slice mushrooms, carrots, and tofu into appropriate sizes.
   - Cut napa cabbage and bok choy (or spinach) into bite-sized pieces.
3. **Cook the Hot Pot:**
   - Bring the broth to a gentle simmer at the table or on the stove.

- Add the chicken pieces and cook until fully cooked, about 5-7 minutes.
- Add the carrots, mushrooms, and tofu (if using). Simmer until the vegetables are tender, about 10 minutes.
- Add the napa cabbage and bok choy (or spinach) in the last few minutes of cooking.

4. **Add Noodles (Optional):**
   - If using noodles, cook them separately according to package instructions, then add them to the hot pot to heat through just before serving.

5. **Serve:**
   - Divide the hot pot ingredients and broth between serving bowls.
   - Garnish with sliced green onions, shichimi togarashi, sesame seeds, and fresh herbs if desired.

Tips:

- **Broth:** You can make the broth richer by simmering it with kombu (dried kelp) or adding a little more soy sauce and mirin according to your taste.
- **Chicken:** Boneless chicken thighs are ideal because they remain tender and flavorful. You can use bone-in chicken pieces for a richer broth.
- **Vegetables:** Feel free to customize the vegetables based on your preference or what's in season. Other additions might include daikon radish, corn, or snow peas.

Tori Nabe is a versatile and hearty dish perfect for family dinners or gatherings. Enjoy the comforting flavors and the communal experience of sharing a hot pot meal!

Motsunabe

Ingredients:

For the Broth:

- **4 cups dashi broth** (or chicken/vegetable broth with dashi powder)
- **1/4 cup soy sauce**
- **1/4 cup miso paste** (white or red, depending on your preference)
- **2 tablespoons mirin** (sweet rice wine)
- **2 tablespoons sake** (Japanese rice wine, optional)
- **1 tablespoon sugar** (adjust to taste)

For the Hot Pot:

- **1 lb (450g) beef or pork offal** (such as tripe, cleaned and cut into bite-sized pieces)
- **2 tablespoons vegetable oil**
- **1 large onion** (sliced thinly)
- **3-4 cloves garlic** (sliced thinly)
- **1-inch piece of ginger** (sliced thinly)
- **1 cup mushrooms** (shiitake, enoki, or other varieties)
- **1-2 carrots** (peeled and sliced into rounds)
- **1 cup cabbage** (cut into bite-sized pieces)
- **1 cup bean sprouts**
- **1 block tofu** (cut into cubes, optional)
- **2-3 green onions** (sliced)
- **1-2 sheets kombu (dried kelp)** (optional, for extra umami)
- **1 cup Chinese cabbage or napa cabbage** (cut into bite-sized pieces)

For Garnish:

- **Chopped green onions**
- **Chili pepper flakes** (optional, for added spice)
- **Shichimi togarashi** (Japanese seven-spice blend, optional)
- **Fresh herbs** (such as cilantro or parsley, optional)

Instructions:

1. **Prepare the Broth:**
   - In a large pot, combine dashi broth (or chicken/vegetable broth with dashi powder), soy sauce, miso paste, mirin, sake (if using), and sugar. Stir well and bring to a simmer. Adjust seasoning to taste and keep warm.
2. **Prepare the Offal:**

- Rinse the beef or pork offal under cold water and pat dry. Cut into bite-sized pieces if needed.
3. **Cook the Aromatics:**
    - Heat vegetable oil in a large pot or Dutch oven over medium-high heat.
    - Add the sliced onions, garlic, and ginger. Sauté until fragrant and the onions are translucent, about 3-4 minutes.
4. **Add the Offal:**
    - Add the offal to the pot and cook until it starts to brown, about 5 minutes.
5. **Add the Broth:**
    - Pour the prepared broth over the offal in the pot. Add kombu (if using) and bring to a simmer.
6. **Simmer:**
    - Simmer the mixture for about 30 minutes, or until the offal is tender and the flavors have melded. Skim off any impurities that rise to the surface.
7. **Add Vegetables:**
    - Add the mushrooms, carrots, cabbage, bean sprouts, and tofu (if using). Simmer for an additional 10-15 minutes, or until the vegetables are tender.
8. **Serve:**
    - Ladle the Motsunabe into individual bowls or serve directly from the pot at the table.
    - Garnish with chopped green onions, chili pepper flakes, shichimi togarashi, and fresh herbs if desired.

Tips:

- **Offal Preparation:** Ensure the offal is thoroughly cleaned and blanched before adding it to the pot to remove any impurities and strong flavors.
- **Broth:** Adjust the saltiness or sweetness of the broth according to your taste. You can add more soy sauce or sugar if needed.
- **Vegetables:** Customize the vegetables based on your preferences or what's in season. Additional vegetables like bell peppers or sweet corn can also be added.

Motsunabe is a hearty and flavorful dish perfect for warming up during colder months or for enjoying with friends and family. The combination of tender offal, savory broth, and fresh vegetables makes it a satisfying and memorable meal!

Kake Udon

Ingredients:

For the Broth:

- **4 cups dashi broth** (or chicken/vegetable broth with dashi powder)
- **1/4 cup soy sauce**
- **2 tablespoons mirin** (sweet rice wine)
- **1 tablespoon sake** (Japanese rice wine, optional)
- **1 tablespoon sugar** (adjust to taste)

For the Udon:

- **200-300g udon noodles** (fresh or dried)
- **2-3 green onions** (sliced thinly)
- **1 sheet nori (seaweed)** (cut into strips, optional)
- **Shredded tempura** (optional, for garnish)
- **Pickled ginger** (optional, for garnish)

Instructions:

1. **Prepare the Broth:**
    - In a large pot, combine dashi broth (or chicken/vegetable broth with dashi powder), soy sauce, mirin, sake (if using), and sugar. Stir well and bring to a simmer. Adjust the seasoning to taste and keep warm.
2. **Cook the Udon Noodles:**
    - Cook the udon noodles according to the package instructions. Fresh udon typically takes about 3-5 minutes, while dried udon may take 7-10 minutes.
    - Once cooked, drain the noodles and rinse them under cold water to stop the cooking process. Set aside.
3. **Assemble the Dish:**
    - Divide the cooked udon noodles into serving bowls.
    - Ladle the hot broth over the noodles.
4. **Garnish and Serve:**
    - Garnish with sliced green onions, nori strips, shredded tempura, and pickled ginger if desired.
    - Serve hot and enjoy!

Tips:

- **Broth:** For a richer flavor, you can simmer the broth for a longer time or add a little more soy sauce and mirin to suit your taste.

- **Noodles:** If using dried udon noodles, be sure to cook them thoroughly and rinse them to remove excess starch. Fresh udon is preferred for its superior texture, but dried udon works well too.
- **Garnishes:** Customize the garnishes based on your preferences. Tempura, mushrooms, or a soft-boiled egg can also be great additions.

Kake Udon is a comforting and versatile dish that's perfect for a quick meal or a cozy dinner. Enjoy the warm, soothing broth and the chewy udon noodles in this classic Japanese dish!

Koya Dofu Stew

Ingredients:

For the Stew:

- **1 package koya dofu** (dried tofu, about 100g, soaked in water to rehydrate)
- **1 tablespoon vegetable oil**
- **1 large onion** (sliced thinly)
- **2-3 cloves garlic** (minced)
- **1-inch piece of ginger** (grated or minced)
- **2 carrots** (peeled and sliced into rounds)
- **1 cup mushrooms** (shiitake, enoki, or other varieties)
- **1 cup napa cabbage** (cut into bite-sized pieces)
- **1 cup daikon radish** (peeled and sliced)
- **1 block of tofu** (cubed, optional for added texture)
- **2-3 green onions** (sliced thinly, for garnish)

For the Broth:

- **4 cups dashi broth** (or chicken/vegetable broth with dashi powder)
- **1/4 cup soy sauce**
- **2 tablespoons mirin** (sweet rice wine)
- **2 tablespoons sake** (Japanese rice wine, optional)
- **1 tablespoon sugar** (adjust to taste)

For Garnish:

- **Chopped green onions**
- **Shredded nori (seaweed)** (optional)
- **Shichimi togarashi** (Japanese seven-spice blend, optional)

Instructions:

1. **Prepare the Koya Dofu:**
    - Soak the koya dofu in warm water for 15-20 minutes, or until it becomes soft and rehydrated. Drain and gently squeeze out excess water. Cut into bite-sized pieces.
2. **Prepare the Broth:**
    - In a large pot, combine dashi broth (or chicken/vegetable broth with dashi powder), soy sauce, mirin, sake (if using), and sugar. Stir well and bring to a simmer. Adjust seasoning to taste.
3. **Cook the Aromatics:**

- Heat vegetable oil in the same pot over medium heat.
- Add the sliced onion, garlic, and ginger. Sauté until fragrant and the onions are translucent, about 5 minutes.

4. **Add Vegetables and Koya Dofu:**
   - Add carrots, mushrooms, daikon radish, and rehydrated koya dofu to the pot. Stir to combine.
   - Pour the prepared broth over the vegetables and koya dofu. Bring to a boil.

5. **Simmer:**
   - Reduce heat to low, cover, and simmer for 20-30 minutes, or until the vegetables are tender and the flavors have melded. If using fresh tofu, add it in the last 10 minutes of cooking to warm through.

6. **Serve:**
   - Ladle the stew into serving bowls.
   - Garnish with sliced green onions, shredded nori, and a sprinkle of shichimi togarashi if desired.

Tips:

- **Koya Dofu:** Ensure that koya dofu is thoroughly soaked and rehydrated before cooking. It will absorb the flavors of the broth, making it a key component of the stew.
- **Broth:** Adjust the sweetness or saltiness of the broth by adding more sugar or soy sauce according to your taste.
- **Vegetables:** Feel free to customize the vegetables based on your preferences or what's in season.

Koya Dofu Stew is a hearty and nourishing dish that brings out the unique texture and flavor of dried tofu. Enjoy this warming stew as a satisfying meal during the colder months!

Tori Dango Soup

Ingredients:

For the Chicken Meatballs:

- **1 lb (450g) ground chicken** (preferably thigh for more flavor)
- **1/4 cup panko breadcrumbs** (Japanese breadcrumbs)
- **1/4 cup finely chopped scallions**
- **1 egg** (lightly beaten)
- **2 tablespoons soy sauce**
- **1 tablespoon mirin** (sweet rice wine)
- **1 tablespoon sake** (Japanese rice wine, optional)
- **1 teaspoon grated ginger**
- **1 teaspoon sesame oil** (optional)

For the Soup:

- **4 cups chicken broth** (or dashi broth)
- **2-3 cups vegetables** (e.g., sliced mushrooms, carrots, napa cabbage, bok choy, or daikon radish)
- **1 tablespoon soy sauce**
- **1 tablespoon mirin** (sweet rice wine)
- **1 tablespoon sake** (Japanese rice wine, optional)
- **1 teaspoon grated ginger** (optional, for added flavor)

For Garnish:

- **Chopped green onions**
- **Shredded nori (seaweed)**
- **Fresh herbs** (such as cilantro or parsley, optional)

Instructions:

1. **Prepare the Chicken Meatballs:**
    - In a large bowl, combine ground chicken, panko breadcrumbs, finely chopped scallions, beaten egg, soy sauce, mirin, sake (if using), grated ginger, and sesame oil (if using).
    - Mix well until all ingredients are fully incorporated. Wet your hands slightly to prevent sticking, then form the mixture into bite-sized meatballs, about 1 inch in diameter.
2. **Prepare the Soup:**
    - In a large pot, bring chicken broth (or dashi broth) to a simmer over medium heat.

- Add soy sauce, mirin, and sake (if using). Stir to combine.
3. **Cook the Meatballs:**
   - Gently drop the prepared meatballs into the simmering broth. Cook for about 5-7 minutes, or until the meatballs are fully cooked and float to the surface.
4. **Add Vegetables:**
   - Add your choice of vegetables (e.g., mushrooms, carrots, napa cabbage, bok choy, or daikon radish) to the pot. Simmer for an additional 5-10 minutes, or until the vegetables are tender.
5. **Adjust Seasoning:**
   - Taste the broth and adjust seasoning with additional soy sauce, mirin, or salt if needed. Add grated ginger if using.
6. **Serve:**
   - Ladle the soup into bowls, making sure each bowl gets a few meatballs and a good amount of vegetables.
   - Garnish with chopped green onions, shredded nori, and fresh herbs if desired.

Tips:

- **Chicken Meatballs:** For a lighter texture, use a mix of chicken breast and thigh or add a little grated daikon radish to the mixture.
- **Vegetables:** Customize the vegetables based on your preferences and what's in season. Be sure to cut them into bite-sized pieces to ensure even cooking.
- **Broth:** If you prefer a richer flavor, you can use homemade chicken broth or add a splash of soy sauce or miso for extra depth.

Tori Dango Soup is a versatile and hearty dish that provides warmth and comfort. The tender chicken meatballs and flavorful broth make it a delicious and satisfying meal. Enjoy this comforting soup with family and friends!

Salmon Nabe

Ingredients:

For the Broth:

- **4 cups dashi broth** (or chicken/vegetable broth with dashi powder)
- **1/4 cup soy sauce**
- **2 tablespoons mirin** (sweet rice wine)
- **2 tablespoons sake** (Japanese rice wine, optional)
- **1 tablespoon sugar** (adjust to taste)

For the Hot Pot:

- **1 lb (450g) salmon fillets** (cut into bite-sized pieces)
- **1 cup mushrooms** (shiitake, enoki, or other varieties)
- **1-2 carrots** (peeled and sliced into rounds)
- **1 cup napa cabbage** (cut into bite-sized pieces)
- **1 cup bok choy** (or spinach)
- **1 block tofu** (cut into cubes, optional)
- **2-3 green onions** (sliced thinly)
- **1-2 sheets kombu (dried kelp)** (optional, for extra umami)
- **1 cup udon noodles** (or soba/ramen, optional)

For Garnish:

- **Chopped green onions**
- **Shredded nori (seaweed)**
- **Shichimi togarashi** (Japanese seven-spice blend, optional)
- **Fresh herbs** (such as cilantro or parsley, optional)

Instructions:

1. **Prepare the Broth:**
   - In a large pot, combine dashi broth (or chicken/vegetable broth with dashi powder), soy sauce, mirin, sake (if using), and sugar. Stir well and bring to a simmer. Adjust seasoning to taste and keep warm.
2. **Prepare the Salmon:**
   - Cut the salmon fillets into bite-sized pieces.
3. **Prepare the Vegetables:**
   - Slice the mushrooms, carrots, and tofu (if using) into appropriate sizes.
   - Cut napa cabbage and bok choy (or spinach) into bite-sized pieces.
4. **Cook the Hot Pot:**

- Bring the broth to a gentle simmer on the stove or at the table if using a portable burner.
- Add the salmon pieces and cook for about 5-7 minutes, or until the salmon is cooked through and flakes easily.

5. **Add Vegetables:**
    - Add mushrooms, carrots, tofu (if using), napa cabbage, and bok choy (or spinach) to the pot.
    - Simmer for an additional 5-10 minutes, or until the vegetables are tender.
6. **Add Noodles (Optional):**
    - If using noodles, cook them separately according to package instructions, then add them to the hot pot to heat through just before serving.
7. **Serve:**
    - Ladle the hot pot contents into individual bowls, making sure each bowl gets a portion of salmon, vegetables, and broth.
    - Garnish with sliced green onions, shredded nori, and shichimi togarashi if desired.

Tips:

- **Salmon:** Use fresh salmon fillets for the best flavor. If you prefer, you can use salmon belly or other parts of the fish for added richness.
- **Broth:** Adjust the broth's seasoning to your taste. You can add more soy sauce or mirin if needed.
- **Vegetables:** Feel free to add other vegetables like mushrooms, snow peas, or baby corn according to your preference or what you have on hand.

Salmon Nabe is a warm and hearty dish that's perfect for sharing with family and friends. The combination of tender salmon, flavorful broth, and fresh vegetables makes it a comforting and delicious meal. Enjoy!

Daikon Radish Soup

Ingredients:

For the Soup:

- **1 large daikon radish** (peeled and sliced into thin rounds or half-moons)
- **1-2 carrots** (peeled and sliced into thin rounds)
- **1 cup mushrooms** (shiitake, enoki, or other varieties, sliced)
- **1 block tofu** (cubed, optional)
- **2-3 green onions** (sliced thinly)
- **1 tablespoon vegetable oil**
- **4 cups dashi broth** (or chicken/vegetable broth with dashi powder)
- **2 tablespoons soy sauce**
- **1 tablespoon mirin** (sweet rice wine)
- **1 tablespoon sake** (Japanese rice wine, optional)
- **1 teaspoon grated ginger** (optional)

For Garnish:

- **Chopped green onions**
- **Shredded nori (seaweed)**
- **Fresh herbs** (such as cilantro or parsley, optional)
- **Shichimi togarashi** (Japanese seven-spice blend, optional)

Instructions:

1. **Prepare the Daikon and Vegetables:**
   - Peel and slice the daikon radish into thin rounds or half-moons. Slice the carrots and mushrooms as well. If using tofu, cut it into cubes.
2. **Cook the Aromatics:**
   - Heat vegetable oil in a large pot over medium heat.
   - Add the sliced green onions and cook for a few minutes until they are fragrant but not browned.
3. **Add Vegetables:**
   - Add the sliced daikon radish, carrots, and mushrooms to the pot. Sauté for 3-4 minutes to lightly cook the vegetables and enhance their flavors.
4. **Prepare the Broth:**
   - Pour the dashi broth (or chicken/vegetable broth) over the vegetables in the pot. Stir well.
   - Add soy sauce, mirin, sake (if using), and grated ginger (if using). Stir to combine.
5. **Simmer:**

- Bring the soup to a boil, then reduce the heat to low. Simmer for about 15-20 minutes, or until the daikon radish and carrots are tender.
6. **Add Tofu (Optional):**
    - If using tofu, gently add the cubes to the soup and heat through for an additional 5 minutes.
7. **Serve:**
    - Ladle the soup into bowls.
    - Garnish with chopped green onions, shredded nori, and fresh herbs if desired. A sprinkle of shichimi togarashi can add a nice touch of spice.

Tips:

- **Daikon Radish:** Ensure the daikon is sliced thinly and evenly to ensure it cooks evenly and absorbs the flavors of the broth.
- **Broth:** Adjust the seasoning of the broth according to your taste. You can add more soy sauce or mirin if you prefer a stronger flavor.
- **Vegetables:** Feel free to add other vegetables like snow peas, baby corn, or mushrooms based on your preference or availability.

Daikon Radish Soup is a light and nourishing dish that highlights the delicate flavors of daikon. Enjoy this healthy and satisfying soup as a part of your meal!

Chashu Ramen

Ingredients:

For the Chashu:

- **1 lb (450g) pork belly** (skin-on, if possible)
- **1/4 cup soy sauce**
- **1/4 cup mirin** (sweet rice wine)
- **1/4 cup sake** (Japanese rice wine)
- **1/4 cup sugar**
- **2 cups water**
- **2 cloves garlic** (crushed)
- **1-inch piece of ginger** (sliced)
- **1-2 green onions** (chopped)
- **1 star anise** (optional)

For the Ramen:

- **4 cups chicken or pork broth** (or dashi)
- **2 tablespoons soy sauce**
- **1 tablespoon miso paste** (optional, for extra depth)
- **1 tablespoon mirin**
- **2-3 cloves garlic** (minced)
- **1-inch piece of ginger** (grated)
- **2 servings ramen noodles** (fresh or dried)
- **1-2 green onions** (sliced thinly, for garnish)
- **1 cup mushrooms** (shiitake or other varieties, sliced, optional)
- **1 cup bok choy** (or spinach, optional)
- **1 sheet nori (seaweed)** (cut into strips, optional)
- **1-2 eggs** (soft-boiled, optional)

Instructions:

1. **Prepare the Chashu:**
   - Roll the pork belly into a log shape and tie it tightly with kitchen twine. This helps it hold its shape during cooking.
   - In a large pot or Dutch oven, combine soy sauce, mirin, sake, sugar, water, garlic, ginger, green onions, and star anise (if using). Stir to combine.
   - Add the pork belly to the pot. Bring to a boil, then reduce the heat to low. Cover and simmer for 2-3 hours, turning the pork occasionally, until it is tender and the flavors are absorbed.
2. **Prepare the Ramen Broth:**

- In a separate pot, heat a little oil over medium heat and sauté garlic and ginger until fragrant.
- Add chicken or pork broth to the pot and bring to a simmer.
- Stir in soy sauce, miso paste (if using), and mirin. Simmer for 10 minutes. Adjust seasoning to taste.

3. **Cook the Ramen Noodles:**
   - Cook the ramen noodles according to the package instructions. Drain and set aside.

4. **Prepare Toppings:**
   - Slice the chashu into thin rounds.
   - If using, sauté mushrooms and blanch bok choy.

5. **Assemble the Ramen:**
   - Divide the cooked ramen noodles into bowls.
   - Ladle the hot broth over the noodles.
   - Top with slices of chashu, mushrooms, bok choy, and any additional toppings you like (e.g., soft-boiled eggs, nori).

6. **Serve:**
   - Garnish with sliced green onions and any other desired toppings.
   - Serve hot and enjoy!

Tips:

- **Chashu:** For the best results, let the chashu cool in its braising liquid before slicing. This helps the meat retain its juices and makes slicing easier.
- **Broth:** Feel free to customize the broth by adding other seasonings or ingredients according to your taste.
- **Noodles:** Fresh ramen noodles are ideal, but dried noodles work well too. Cook them just before serving to maintain their texture.

Chashu Ramen is a rich and satisfying dish that brings together tender pork belly, flavorful broth, and delicious ramen noodles. Enjoy this classic Japanese favorite!

Tofu and Vegetable Hot Pot

Ingredients:

For the Broth:

- **4 cups dashi broth** (or chicken/vegetable broth with dashi powder)
- **1/4 cup soy sauce**
- **2 tablespoons mirin** (sweet rice wine)
- **2 tablespoons sake** (Japanese rice wine, optional)
- **1 tablespoon sugar** (adjust to taste)
- **1-2 cloves garlic** (minced, optional)
- **1-inch piece of ginger** (grated, optional)

For the Hot Pot:

- **1 block of firm tofu** (cut into cubes)
- **1 cup mushrooms** (shiitake, enoki, or other varieties, sliced)
- **1-2 carrots** (peeled and sliced into rounds or thin strips)
- **1 cup napa cabbage** (cut into bite-sized pieces)
- **1 cup bok choy** (or spinach)
- **1 cup daikon radish** (peeled and sliced into rounds)
- **1 cup snow peas** (or sugar snap peas)
- **2-3 green onions** (sliced thinly)
- **1 sheet nori (seaweed)** (cut into strips, optional)
- **1-2 tablespoons sesame oil** (for drizzling, optional)

For Garnish:

- **Chopped green onions**
- **Shredded nori (seaweed)**
- **Fresh herbs** (such as cilantro or parsley, optional)
- **Shichimi togarashi** (Japanese seven-spice blend, optional)

Instructions:

1. **Prepare the Broth:**
   - In a large pot, combine dashi broth (or chicken/vegetable broth with dashi powder), soy sauce, mirin, sake (if using), and sugar. Stir well and bring to a simmer.
   - If using garlic and ginger, add them to the pot and simmer for 5 minutes to infuse the flavors. Adjust seasoning to taste.
2. **Prepare the Vegetables and Tofu:**

- Cut the tofu into bite-sized cubes and set aside.
- Slice the mushrooms, carrots, daikon radish, and green onions. Cut the napa cabbage and bok choy into bite-sized pieces.

3. **Cook the Hot Pot:**
   - Bring the broth to a gentle simmer over medium heat.
   - Add the daikon radish and carrots to the pot and cook for about 5-7 minutes until they start to soften.
   - Add the mushrooms, napa cabbage, bok choy, and snow peas. Simmer for another 5 minutes until the vegetables are tender.

4. **Add Tofu:**
   - Gently add the tofu cubes to the pot and simmer for an additional 5 minutes to heat through.

5. **Serve:**
   - Ladle the hot pot into individual bowls or serve directly from the pot at the table.
   - Garnish with sliced green onions, shredded nori, and fresh herbs if desired.
   - Drizzle with sesame oil for extra flavor, if using.

6. **Optional:**
   - You can serve the hot pot with steamed rice or noodles for a more substantial meal.

Tips:

- **Tofu:** Use firm or extra-firm tofu for better texture. Silken tofu can be too delicate and may break apart during cooking.
- **Vegetables:** Customize the vegetables based on your preference or what's in season. You can also add other ingredients like tofu skin, mushrooms, or baby corn.
- **Broth:** Adjust the seasoning of the broth to your taste. You can add more soy sauce or a pinch of salt if needed.

Tofu and Vegetable Hot Pot is a versatile and comforting dish that's both healthy and satisfying. Enjoy the rich flavors and variety of textures in this delightful Japanese hot pot!

Hōba Miso Grilled Fish

Ingredients:

For the Miso Paste:

- **1/4 cup miso paste** (white or red miso, depending on your preference)
- **2 tablespoons mirin** (sweet rice wine)
- **1 tablespoon sake** (Japanese rice wine)
- **1 tablespoon sugar**
- **1 tablespoon soy sauce**

For the Fish:

- **4 pieces of white fish fillets** (e.g., cod, halibut, or sea bass, about 6 oz each)
- **Hōba leaves** (or banana leaves/foil if hōba leaves are unavailable)
- **1 tablespoon vegetable oil** (for brushing)

For Garnish:

- **Chopped green onions**
- **Shredded nori (seaweed)**
- **Sesame seeds**
- **Lemon wedges** (optional)

Instructions:

1. **Prepare the Miso Paste:**
   - In a small bowl, combine miso paste, mirin, sake, sugar, and soy sauce. Mix well until smooth and the sugar is fully dissolved. Set aside.
2. **Prepare the Fish:**
   - Pat the fish fillets dry with paper towels.
   - Brush each fillet with the miso paste mixture, ensuring it's coated evenly.
3. **Wrap in Hōba Leaves:**
   - If using hōba leaves, clean them thoroughly and lightly brush them with vegetable oil to prevent sticking.
   - Wrap each miso-coated fish fillet in a hōba leaf, securing with toothpicks if necessary. If using banana leaves or foil, wrap the fish tightly.
4. **Grill the Fish:**
   - Preheat a grill or grill pan to medium heat.
   - Place the wrapped fish on the grill and cook for 8-10 minutes per side, or until the fish is cooked through and flakes easily with a fork. The cooking time may vary depending on the thickness of the fillets and the heat of the grill.

5. **Serve:**
    - Carefully unwrap the fish from the leaves or foil.
    - Transfer to serving plates and garnish with chopped green onions, shredded nori, and sesame seeds.
    - Serve with lemon wedges if desired.

Tips:

- **Miso Paste:** Adjust the amount of sugar and soy sauce in the miso paste to suit your taste. For a sweeter flavor, increase the sugar; for a saltier taste, add more soy sauce.
- **Fish:** Choose a firm, white fish for best results. Ensure the fish is fresh for optimal flavor and texture.
- **Hōba Leaves:** If using hōba leaves, ensure they are clean and free of any dirt. Lightly oiling the leaves helps to prevent the fish from sticking.

Hōba Miso Grilled Fish offers a delicious blend of savory miso and aromatic hōba leaves, creating a memorable dish that highlights the best of Japanese flavors. Enjoy this flavorful and visually appealing grilled fish!

Paitan Ramen

Ingredients:

For the Broth:

- **2 lbs (900g) chicken bones** (preferably with some meat still attached)
- **1 lb (450g) pork bones** (optional, for added richness)
- **1 onion** (quartered)
- **1 carrot** (peeled and cut into chunks)
- **1-2 cloves garlic** (crushed)
- **1-inch piece of ginger** (sliced)
- **4-6 cups water** (adjust as needed)

For the Tare (Seasoning Sauce):

- **1/4 cup soy sauce**
- **1/4 cup mirin** (sweet rice wine)
- **1 tablespoon sake** (Japanese rice wine, optional)
- **1 tablespoon sugar** (adjust to taste)
- **1-2 cloves garlic** (minced, optional)
- **1-inch piece of ginger** (grated, optional)

For the Ramen:

- **2 servings ramen noodles** (fresh or dried)
- **1 cup cooked chicken** (shredded or sliced, optional)
- **1-2 green onions** (sliced thinly)
- **1 cup mushrooms** (shiitake or other varieties, sliced, optional)
- **1-2 soft-boiled eggs** (optional)
- **1 cup bean sprouts** (optional)
- **1 sheet nori (seaweed)** (cut into strips, optional)
- **Sesame seeds** (for garnish, optional)

Instructions:

1. **Prepare the Broth:**
    - Place the chicken bones and pork bones (if using) in a large pot. Cover with cold water and bring to a boil over high heat.
    - Once boiling, drain the bones and discard the water. This step helps to remove impurities and ensures a cleaner broth.
    - Rinse the bones under cold water to remove any remaining residue.

- Return the bones to the pot and cover with fresh cold water. Add the onion, carrot, garlic, and ginger.
- Bring to a boil again, then reduce the heat to low. Simmer gently for 4-6 hours, or until the broth becomes milky and opaque. Add more water as needed to keep the bones covered.
- Strain the broth through a fine mesh sieve into another pot, discarding the solids.

2. **Prepare the Tare:**
   - In a small saucepan, combine soy sauce, mirin, sake (if using), and sugar. Heat gently until the sugar is dissolved. Add minced garlic and grated ginger if using.
   - Set aside to cool.

3. **Cook the Ramen Noodles:**
   - Cook the ramen noodles according to the package instructions. Drain and set aside.

4. **Assemble the Ramen:**
   - Reheat the strained broth and adjust seasoning if necessary.
   - Place a small amount of tare into each serving bowl (about 1-2 tablespoons, adjust to taste).
   - Add the hot broth to the bowls over the tare, stirring to combine.
   - Add the cooked noodles to the bowls.

5. **Add Toppings:**
   - Top with cooked chicken, sliced green onions, mushrooms, soft-boiled eggs, bean sprouts, and nori strips as desired.
   - Garnish with sesame seeds if desired.

6. **Serve:**
   - Serve immediately and enjoy your rich and creamy Paitan Ramen!

Tips:

- **Broth:** The key to a great paitan ramen broth is a long simmering time to extract maximum flavor and richness from the bones.
- **Tare:** Adjust the amount of tare based on your taste preferences. You can also experiment with other seasonings like miso or oyster sauce.
- **Noodles:** Fresh ramen noodles are preferred for the best texture, but dried noodles will work too. Cook them just before serving to maintain their texture.

Paitan Ramen is a hearty and satisfying dish that showcases the rich, creamy texture of its broth. Enjoy this delicious ramen with all your favorite toppings for a truly comforting meal!

Chicken Karage

Ingredients:

For the Marinade:

- **1 lb (450g) boneless, skinless chicken thighs** (cut into bite-sized pieces)
- **2 tablespoons soy sauce**
- **2 tablespoons sake** (Japanese rice wine, or white wine as a substitute)
- **1 tablespoon mirin** (sweet rice wine)
- **1 tablespoon grated ginger**
- **2 cloves garlic** (minced)
- **1 teaspoon sugar** (optional, adjust to taste)

For Coating and Frying:

- **1/2 cup all-purpose flour**
- **1/4 cup cornstarch**
- **1/2 teaspoon baking powder** (optional, for extra crispiness)
- **Salt and pepper** (to taste)
- **Vegetable oil** (for deep-frying)

For Garnish (optional):

- **Lemon wedges**
- **Shredded cabbage**
- **Chopped green onions**

Instructions:

1. **Marinate the Chicken:**
    - In a bowl, combine soy sauce, sake, mirin, grated ginger, minced garlic, and sugar.
    - Add the chicken pieces to the marinade and mix well to ensure the chicken is evenly coated. Cover and refrigerate for at least 30 minutes to 1 hour. For best results, marinate overnight.
2. **Prepare the Coating:**
    - In a separate bowl, mix together flour, cornstarch, baking powder (if using), salt, and pepper.
    - Remove the chicken pieces from the marinade, letting any excess liquid drip off.
    - Dredge each piece of chicken in the flour mixture, ensuring it's coated evenly. Shake off any excess.
3. **Heat the Oil:**

- Heat vegetable oil in a deep fryer or large skillet to 350°F (175°C). If using a skillet, make sure there's enough oil to submerge the chicken pieces halfway.
4. **Fry the Chicken:**
    - Carefully add a few pieces of chicken to the hot oil, being careful not to overcrowd the pan. Fry in batches if necessary.
    - Cook the chicken for 4-6 minutes, or until golden brown and crispy. The internal temperature should reach 165°F (75°C).
    - Use a slotted spoon to remove the chicken from the oil and drain on paper towels.
5. **Serve:**
    - Serve the crispy chicken karaage hot, garnished with lemon wedges, shredded cabbage, and chopped green onions if desired.

Tips:

- **Marinating:** Marinate the chicken for as long as possible to enhance the flavor. Even a short marination time will improve the taste.
- **Coating:** Ensure the chicken is evenly coated in the flour mixture for a consistent crunch.
- **Oil Temperature:** Maintain the oil temperature to ensure the chicken cooks evenly and becomes crispy. If the oil is too hot, the outside will burn before the inside cooks; if too cool, the chicken will be greasy.
- **Double Frying:** For extra crispiness, you can fry the chicken twice. After the first fry, let it rest for a few minutes, then fry it again for an additional 1-2 minutes.

Chicken Karaage is a delightful treat that's loved for its crunchy exterior and juicy interior. Enjoy this flavorful dish as a snack, appetizer, or part of a larger meal!

Agedashi Tofu

Ingredients:

For the Tofu:

- **1 block of firm or extra-firm tofu** (about 14 oz, cut into 1-inch cubes)
- **1/2 cup cornstarch** (or potato starch)
- **Vegetable oil** (for deep-frying)

For the Broth:

- **2 cups dashi broth** (or chicken/vegetable broth with dashi powder)
- **1/4 cup soy sauce**
- **1/4 cup mirin** (sweet rice wine)
- **1 tablespoon sake** (Japanese rice wine, optional)
- **1 tablespoon sugar** (optional, adjust to taste)

For Garnish:

- **Chopped green onions**
- **Grated daikon radish** (optional)
- **Shredded nori (seaweed)** (optional)
- **Pickled ginger** (optional)

Instructions:

1. **Prepare the Tofu:**
   - Drain the tofu and pat it dry with paper towels to remove excess moisture. Press the tofu gently to expel any remaining liquid.
   - Cut the tofu into 1-inch cubes.
2. **Coat the Tofu:**
   - Place the cornstarch in a shallow dish. Lightly coat each tofu cube with cornstarch, shaking off any excess. This will help create a crispy exterior.
3. **Heat the Oil:**
   - In a deep fryer or large skillet, heat vegetable oil to 350°F (175°C). If using a skillet, ensure there's enough oil to submerge the tofu cubes halfway.
4. **Fry the Tofu:**
   - Carefully add the tofu cubes to the hot oil in batches, being careful not to overcrowd the pan.
   - Fry the tofu for 3-4 minutes, or until golden brown and crispy. Use a slotted spoon to remove the tofu from the oil and drain on paper towels.
5. **Prepare the Broth:**

- In a saucepan, combine dashi broth, soy sauce, mirin, sake (if using), and sugar (if using). Bring to a simmer over medium heat and cook for 2-3 minutes to blend the flavors.

6. **Assemble the Dish:**
    - Place the fried tofu cubes in serving bowls.
    - Pour the hot broth over the tofu.
    - Garnish with chopped green onions, grated daikon radish, shredded nori, and pickled ginger if desired.
7. **Serve:**
    - Serve immediately while the tofu is still crispy and the broth is hot.

Tips:

- **Tofu:** Firm or extra-firm tofu works best for this dish as it holds its shape during frying.
- **Broth:** Adjust the sweetness and saltiness of the broth according to your taste. You can add more sugar or soy sauce if needed.
- **Oil Temperature:** Make sure the oil is at the right temperature to ensure the tofu becomes crispy. Too hot and the tofu will burn; too cool and it will absorb excess oil.
- **Double Frying:** For extra crispiness, you can double fry the tofu. Fry the tofu once until lightly golden, let it rest, and then fry again for an additional 1-2 minutes.

Agedashi Tofu is a delightful dish with a crispy exterior and a flavorful, savory broth. Enjoy it as an appetizer, side dish, or part of a larger Japanese meal!

Katsu Curry

Ingredients:

For the Katsu (Pork Cutlet):

- **4 boneless pork chops** (about 6 oz each)
- **Salt and pepper** (to taste)
- **1/2 cup all-purpose flour**
- **1 large egg** (beaten)
- **1 cup panko breadcrumbs** (Japanese breadcrumbs)
- **Vegetable oil** (for frying)

For the Curry Sauce:

- **1 tablespoon vegetable oil**
- **1 onion** (finely chopped)
- **2 cloves garlic** (minced)
- **1-inch piece of ginger** (grated)
- **2 carrots** (peeled and sliced)
- **1 potato** (peeled and diced)
- **2-3 cups chicken or vegetable broth**
- **1-2 tablespoons curry powder** (adjust to taste)
- **1 tablespoon soy sauce**
- **1 tablespoon Worcestershire sauce** (optional)
- **1-2 tablespoons sugar** (adjust to taste)
- **1-2 tablespoons flour or cornstarch** (mixed with a little water to make a slurry, optional, for thickening)

For Serving:

- **Cooked white rice**
- **Chopped green onions** (optional)
- **Pickled vegetables** (optional)

Instructions:

1. **Prepare the Katsu:**
     - **Pound the Pork:** Place the pork chops between two sheets of plastic wrap. Gently pound them with a meat mallet or rolling pin to an even thickness.
     - **Season and Bread:** Season the pork chops with salt and pepper. Dredge each piece in flour, shaking off excess. Dip in the beaten egg, then coat thoroughly with panko breadcrumbs.

- **Fry the Pork:** Heat vegetable oil in a large skillet over medium heat to about 350°F (175°C). Fry the breaded pork chops for 4-5 minutes per side, or until golden brown and cooked through. Use a slotted spoon to transfer the cutlets to a paper towel-lined plate to drain.

2. **Prepare the Curry Sauce:**
   - **Sauté Aromatics:** In a large saucepan, heat vegetable oil over medium heat. Add the chopped onion and sauté until softened and lightly browned.
   - **Add Garlic and Ginger:** Stir in the minced garlic and grated ginger. Cook for about 1 minute, until fragrant.
   - **Add Vegetables:** Add the carrots and potato. Cook for 3-4 minutes, stirring occasionally.
   - **Add Broth and Simmer:** Pour in the chicken or vegetable broth. Bring to a boil, then reduce heat to low. Simmer for 15-20 minutes, or until the vegetables are tender.
   - **Add Curry Powder:** Stir in the curry powder, soy sauce, Worcestershire sauce (if using), and sugar. Simmer for an additional 5 minutes.
   - **Thicken Sauce:** If you prefer a thicker sauce, mix flour or cornstarch with a little water to create a slurry. Stir this into the curry sauce and cook for a few more minutes until thickened.

3. **Serve:**
   - **Slice the Katsu:** Slice the fried pork cutlets into strips.
   - **Plate the Dish:** Serve the sliced katsu over cooked white rice, and ladle the curry sauce on top.
   - **Garnish:** Garnish with chopped green onions and pickled vegetables if desired.

Tips:

- **Panko Breadcrumbs:** Panko breadcrumbs are key to achieving the crispy texture. If you can't find them, regular breadcrumbs can be used, but the texture may be less crispy.
- **Curry Powder:** Adjust the amount of curry powder to suit your taste. You can use store-bought Japanese curry roux blocks for a more authentic taste, following package instructions.
- **Vegetables:** Feel free to add other vegetables like bell peppers or mushrooms to the curry sauce.

Katsu Curry is a comforting and flavorful dish that brings together the crispy texture of katsu and the rich, savory taste of Japanese curry. Enjoy this delicious meal with a side of white rice and your favorite garnishes!

Japanese Stewed Pork Belly

Ingredients:

For the Pork Belly:

- **1.5 lbs (700g) pork belly** (cut into 2-inch cubes)
- **1 tablespoon vegetable oil**
- **1-2 cloves garlic** (minced)
- **1-inch piece of ginger** (sliced)
- **2-3 green onions** (cut into 2-inch pieces)
- **1 cup water**
- **1/2 cup soy sauce**
- **1/2 cup mirin** (sweet rice wine)
- **1/4 cup sake** (Japanese rice wine)
- **1/4 cup sugar** (adjust to taste)
- **1 tablespoon sesame oil** (optional, for added flavor)
- **1 tablespoon rice vinegar** (optional, to balance sweetness)

For Garnish (optional):

- **Chopped green onions**
- **Sesame seeds**
- **Pickled vegetables**

Instructions:

1. **Prepare the Pork Belly:**
   - Bring a pot of water to a boil. Add the pork belly cubes and blanch for 2-3 minutes to remove impurities. Drain and rinse the pork under cold water. This step helps to ensure a clean broth and reduces excess fat.
2. **Brown the Pork:**
   - Heat vegetable oil in a large pot or Dutch oven over medium-high heat. Add the pork belly cubes and brown on all sides. This step adds flavor and helps to render some of the fat.
3. **Add Aromatics:**
   - Add minced garlic, sliced ginger, and green onions to the pot. Sauté for 1-2 minutes until fragrant.
4. **Add Liquid and Simmer:**
   - Pour in water, soy sauce, mirin, sake, and sugar. Stir to combine and bring to a simmer.

- Reduce the heat to low, cover, and simmer gently for 1.5 to 2 hours, or until the pork belly is tender and the sauce has thickened. Stir occasionally and skim off any excess fat if needed.

5. **Finish the Dish:**
   - If using, stir in sesame oil and rice vinegar towards the end of cooking. Adjust the seasoning to taste, adding more sugar or soy sauce if desired.
6. **Serve:**
   - Transfer the pork belly and sauce to serving dishes.
   - Garnish with chopped green onions, sesame seeds, and pickled vegetables if desired.
   - Serve with steamed rice or noodles.

Tips:

- **Pork Belly:** Make sure to use well-marbled pork belly for the best texture. The fat is essential for the rich flavor of the dish.
- **Simmering:** Allowing the pork belly to simmer slowly helps to break down the fat and connective tissue, resulting in tender, flavorful meat.
- **Thickening Sauce:** If the sauce is too thin, you can reduce it further by simmering uncovered until it thickens to your desired consistency. Alternatively, mix a small amount of cornstarch with water and stir it into the sauce to thicken.

Japanese Stewed Pork Belly is a delicious and indulgent dish that's perfect for special occasions or a cozy dinner. The tender pork belly and rich, savory-sweet sauce make it a truly satisfying meal. Enjoy!

Shio Ramen

Ingredients:

For the Broth:

- **1 lb (450g) chicken bones** (or a combination of chicken wings and bones)
- **1 onion** (quartered)
- **1 carrot** (peeled and cut into chunks)
- **2 cloves garlic** (crushed)
- **1-inch piece of ginger** (sliced)
- **4-6 cups water**
- **1-2 tablespoons salt** (adjust to taste)

For the Tare (Seasoning Sauce):

- **1/4 cup soy sauce**
- **1 tablespoon sake** (Japanese rice wine, optional)
- **1 tablespoon mirin** (sweet rice wine)
- **1 tablespoon salt** (adjust to taste)

For the Ramen:

- **2 servings fresh or dried ramen noodles**
- **1 cup cooked chicken** (sliced or shredded, optional)
- **1-2 green onions** (sliced thinly)
- **1/2 cup bamboo shoots** (optional)
- **1/2 cup sliced mushrooms** (shiitake or other varieties, optional)
- **1-2 soft-boiled eggs** (optional)
- **Nori (seaweed)** (cut into strips, optional)
- **Bean sprouts** (optional)
- **Sesame seeds** (optional)

Instructions:

1. **Prepare the Broth:**
    - Place the chicken bones, onion, carrot, garlic, and ginger in a large pot. Cover with cold water and bring to a boil over high heat.
    - Once boiling, reduce heat to low and simmer for 1.5 to 2 hours. Skim off any impurities that float to the top.
    - After simmering, strain the broth through a fine mesh sieve into another pot, discarding the solids.
    - Season the broth with salt to taste. Keep warm.

2. **Prepare the Tare:**
   - In a small bowl, combine soy sauce, sake (if using), mirin, and salt. Stir until the salt is dissolved. Adjust seasoning to taste.
3. **Cook the Ramen Noodles:**
   - Cook the ramen noodles according to the package instructions. Drain and set aside.
4. **Assemble the Ramen:**
   - Divide the cooked noodles between serving bowls.
   - Pour the hot broth over the noodles.
   - Add a spoonful of tare to each bowl, adjusting the amount based on your taste preference. Stir to combine.
5. **Add Toppings:**
   - Top each bowl with cooked chicken, sliced green onions, bamboo shoots, mushrooms, soft-boiled eggs, nori strips, bean sprouts, and sesame seeds as desired.
6. **Serve:**
   - Serve immediately while the ramen is hot.

Tips:

- **Broth:** For a clearer broth, make sure to strain it well and remove any fat that has settled on the surface.
- **Noodles:** Fresh ramen noodles are preferred for the best texture, but dried noodles can also be used.
- **Tare:** Adjust the amount of tare according to your taste. You can add more or less based on how salty you like your ramen.
- **Toppings:** Customize the toppings based on your preferences. Traditional options include sliced pork, bamboo shoots, and soft-boiled eggs.

Shio Ramen is a wonderfully light yet flavorful dish that highlights the quality of the broth and noodles. Enjoy the delicate taste and comforting nature of this classic Japanese ramen!

Ramen with Soft-Boiled Egg

Ingredients:

For the Broth:

- **4 cups chicken or vegetable broth** (or use homemade dashi)
- **2 tablespoons soy sauce**
- **1 tablespoon miso paste** (optional, for added depth)
- **1 tablespoon sake** (Japanese rice wine, optional)
- **1 tablespoon mirin** (sweet rice wine)
- **1 teaspoon sugar** (adjust to taste)

For the Toppings:

- **2-4 soft-boiled eggs** (see instructions below)
- **2 servings fresh or dried ramen noodles**
- **1 cup cooked chicken** (sliced or shredded, optional)
- **1-2 green onions** (sliced thinly)
- **1/2 cup bamboo shoots** (optional)
- **1/2 cup sliced mushrooms** (shiitake or other varieties, optional)
- **1/2 cup spinach or bok choy** (optional)
- **Nori (seaweed)** (cut into strips, optional)
- **Bean sprouts** (optional)
- **Sesame seeds** (optional)

Instructions:

1. **Prepare the Broth:**
    - In a pot, combine chicken or vegetable broth, soy sauce, miso paste (if using), sake (if using), mirin, and sugar. Bring to a simmer over medium heat, stirring occasionally until the miso paste and sugar are dissolved.
    - Adjust the seasoning to taste. Keep the broth warm.
2. **Cook the Ramen Noodles:**
    - Cook the ramen noodles according to the package instructions. Drain and rinse under cold water to stop the cooking process. Set aside.
3. **Prepare the Soft-Boiled Eggs:**
    - Bring a pot of water to a boil. Gently add the eggs and cook for 6-7 minutes for a slightly runny yolk or up to 8 minutes for a firmer yolk.
    - Transfer the eggs to a bowl of ice water and let them cool for a few minutes. Peel the eggs carefully once cooled.
4. **Assemble the Ramen:**
    - Divide the cooked noodles between serving bowls.

- Pour the hot broth over the noodles.
- Arrange the toppings over the noodles, including cooked chicken, green onions, bamboo shoots, mushrooms, spinach or bok choy, nori strips, and bean sprouts.

5. **Add the Soft-Boiled Egg:**
    - Cut the soft-boiled eggs in half and place them on top of the ramen. The rich yolk will add a creamy texture to the dish.
6. **Serve:**
    - Garnish with sesame seeds if desired and serve immediately while the ramen is hot.

Tips:

- **Egg Cooking:** For perfectly soft-boiled eggs, use eggs at room temperature and avoid overcooking to ensure a runny yolk.
- **Broth:** Adjust the seasoning of the broth according to your taste. You can add more soy sauce or a bit of salt if needed.
- **Noodles:** Fresh ramen noodles provide the best texture, but dried noodles work well too. Cook them just before serving to keep them from becoming mushy.
- **Toppings:** Feel free to customize the toppings based on your preferences or what you have on hand.

Ramen with Soft-Boiled Egg is a comforting and flavorful meal, with the soft-boiled egg adding a rich and creamy element to the dish. Enjoy this classic Japanese favorite!

Teriyaki Chicken

Ingredients:

For the Chicken:

- **4 boneless, skinless chicken thighs** (or breasts, if preferred)
- **Salt and pepper** (to taste)
- **2 tablespoons vegetable oil** (for cooking)

For the Teriyaki Sauce:

- **1/2 cup soy sauce**
- **1/4 cup mirin** (sweet rice wine)
- **1/4 cup sake** (Japanese rice wine, or white wine as a substitute)
- **2 tablespoons sugar** (adjust to taste)
- **1 tablespoon honey** (optional, for added sweetness)
- **1 tablespoon cornstarch** (mixed with 1 tablespoon water to make a slurry, optional, for thickening)

For Garnish (optional):

- **Chopped green onions**
- **Sesame seeds**
- **Cooked rice** (for serving)
- **Steamed vegetables** (e.g., broccoli, carrots)

Instructions:

1. **Prepare the Teriyaki Sauce:**
   - In a small saucepan, combine soy sauce, mirin, sake, sugar, and honey (if using). Stir to combine.
   - Bring to a simmer over medium heat, stirring occasionally until the sugar is dissolved.
   - If you prefer a thicker sauce, mix cornstarch with water to create a slurry and stir it into the sauce. Continue to simmer for another 1-2 minutes until the sauce thickens. Remove from heat and set aside.
2. **Prepare the Chicken:**
   - Season the chicken thighs with salt and pepper on both sides.
   - Heat vegetable oil in a large skillet over medium-high heat.
   - Add the chicken thighs to the skillet and cook for 5-7 minutes on each side, or until the chicken is cooked through and has a golden-brown crust. The internal temperature should reach 165°F (74°C).

3. **Glaze the Chicken:**
   - Reduce the heat to medium-low. Pour the teriyaki sauce over the cooked chicken in the skillet.
   - Continue to cook for an additional 1-2 minutes, turning the chicken to coat it evenly in the sauce. The sauce will become slightly sticky and glaze the chicken.
4. **Serve:**
   - Remove the chicken from the skillet and let it rest for a few minutes before slicing.
   - Slice the chicken into strips and place it on a serving plate.
   - Drizzle any remaining teriyaki sauce from the skillet over the chicken.
   - Garnish with chopped green onions and sesame seeds if desired.
   - Serve with cooked rice and steamed vegetables.

Tips:

- **Chicken Choice:** Chicken thighs are preferred for their flavor and juiciness, but chicken breasts can also be used. Adjust cooking time as needed.
- **Sauce Thickness:** If you prefer a thicker sauce, let it reduce further on the stove or add more cornstarch slurry.
- **Grilling Option:** For a smoky flavor, you can grill the chicken and brush it with teriyaki sauce during the last few minutes of cooking.
- **Marinating:** For added flavor, marinate the chicken in a portion of the teriyaki sauce before cooking. Reserve some sauce for glazing and serving.

Teriyaki Chicken is a versatile and flavorful dish that's perfect for a quick weeknight dinner or a special meal. Enjoy the sweet and savory glaze with a side of rice and vegetables for a complete and satisfying meal!

Chawanmushi

Ingredients:

For the Egg Mixture:

- **4 large eggs**
- **2 cups dashi broth** (or chicken/vegetable broth as a substitute)
- **2 tablespoons soy sauce**
- **1 tablespoon mirin** (sweet rice wine)
- **1 teaspoon salt** (adjust to taste)

For the Fillings:

- **4-6 small raw shrimp** (peeled and deveined)
- **4-6 small pieces of cooked chicken** (diced)
- **4-6 shiitake mushrooms** (sliced thinly, or use other mushrooms)
- **1/4 cup blanched and sliced ginkgo nuts** (optional)
- **2-3 small slices of kamaboko** (fish cake, optional)
- **2-3 sprigs of fresh parsley or chopped green onions** (for garnish, optional)

Instructions:

1. **Prepare the Fillings:**
   - If using shrimp, blanch them in boiling water for about 1-2 minutes until just cooked. Slice into small pieces if desired.
   - If using mushrooms, sauté them briefly until tender.
2. **Prepare the Egg Mixture:**
   - In a large bowl, whisk together the eggs, dashi broth, soy sauce, mirin, and salt until well combined. Be careful not to create too many bubbles.
   - Strain the mixture through a fine mesh sieve into another bowl to ensure a smooth custard.
3. **Assemble the Chawanmushi:**
   - Divide the prepared fillings among 4 small heatproof cups or ramekins.
   - Gently pour the egg mixture over the fillings, filling each cup about 80% full.
4. **Steam the Chawanmushi:**
   - Prepare a steamer or a pot with a steaming rack. Bring water to a simmer over medium heat.
   - Cover each cup with a lid or aluminum foil to prevent condensation from dripping into the custard.
   - Place the cups in the steamer or on the steaming rack. Steam over low to medium heat for about 15-20 minutes, or until the custard is set. To check for doneness, insert a toothpick or skewer into the center; it should come out clean.

5. **Garnish and Serve:**
    - Once the custards are set, remove them from the steamer and let them cool slightly.
    - Garnish with fresh parsley or chopped green onions if desired.
    - Serve warm.

Tips:

- **Dashi Broth:** Homemade dashi provides the best flavor, but store-bought dashi or other clear broths can also be used.
- **Steaming:** Ensure the water in the steamer is simmering gently and avoid high heat, which can cause bubbles and uneven texture in the custard.
- **Fillings:** You can vary the fillings based on your preferences or what you have on hand. Popular options include crab meat, scallops, or other vegetables.

Chawanmushi is a wonderful dish that combines the silky texture of the custard with the umami flavors of the dashi and soy sauce. It's a delightful and elegant dish that's sure to impress at any meal. Enjoy!

Sweet Potato and Miso Stew

Ingredients:

- **2 tablespoons vegetable oil**
- **1 onion** (diced)
- **2 cloves garlic** (minced)
- **1-inch piece of ginger** (grated)
- **1 large carrot** (peeled and sliced)
- **2 large sweet potatoes** (peeled and cut into bite-sized cubes)
- **4 cups vegetable or chicken broth**
- **2 tablespoons miso paste** (white or red miso, depending on your preference)
- **1 tablespoon soy sauce**
- **1 tablespoon mirin** (sweet rice wine)
- **1 tablespoon sugar** (optional, adjust to taste)
- **1 cup sliced mushrooms** (shiitake, button, or any variety you like)
- **1 cup chopped greens** (such as spinach, bok choy, or kale)
- **Chopped green onions** (for garnish, optional)
- **Sesame seeds** (for garnish, optional)

Instructions:

1. **Prepare the Base:**
    - Heat vegetable oil in a large pot over medium heat. Add the diced onion and cook until translucent, about 5 minutes.
    - Stir in the minced garlic and grated ginger. Cook for an additional 1 minute until fragrant.
2. **Add Vegetables:**
    - Add the sliced carrot and sweet potato cubes to the pot. Stir to combine with the onions, garlic, and ginger.
3. **Add Broth and Simmer:**
    - Pour in the vegetable or chicken broth and bring to a boil. Reduce the heat to low and simmer for about 15-20 minutes, or until the sweet potatoes and carrots are tender.
4. **Prepare the Miso Mixture:**
    - In a small bowl, whisk together the miso paste with a few tablespoons of the hot broth from the pot to loosen it. This helps to ensure the miso mixes smoothly into the stew without clumping.
5. **Add Miso and Seasonings:**
    - Stir the miso mixture into the pot. Add soy sauce, mirin, and sugar (if using). Adjust seasoning to taste. Simmer for an additional 5 minutes to allow the flavors to meld.

6. **Add Mushrooms and Greens:**
    - Add the sliced mushrooms and chopped greens to the pot. Cook for an additional 3-5 minutes, or until the mushrooms are tender and the greens are wilted.
7. **Serve:**
    - Ladle the stew into bowls. Garnish with chopped green onions and sesame seeds if desired. Serve hot.

Tips:

- **Miso:** Adjust the amount of miso paste based on your taste preferences. White miso is milder and sweeter, while red miso has a stronger, saltier flavor.
- **Vegetables:** Feel free to add other vegetables you have on hand, such as bell peppers, potatoes, or zucchini.
- **Thickening:** If you prefer a thicker stew, you can mash some of the sweet potatoes with a spoon or add a slurry made from cornstarch and water.

Sweet Potato and Miso Stew is a warm, nourishing dish that combines sweet and savory flavors in a satisfying stew. It's perfect for a chilly day and pairs well with steamed rice or a side of crusty bread. Enjoy!

Miso Soup with Seaweed

Ingredients:

- **4 cups dashi broth** (or vegetable/chicken broth as a substitute)
- **1/4 cup miso paste** (white or red miso, depending on your preference)
- **1/2 cup dried wakame seaweed** (soaked and drained)
- **1/2 cup tofu** (firm or silken, cut into small cubes)
- **2-3 green onions** (sliced thinly)
- **1-2 cloves garlic** (minced, optional)
- **1 tablespoon soy sauce** (optional, for additional flavor)
- **1 tablespoon mirin** (sweet rice wine, optional)

Instructions:

1. **Prepare the Seaweed:**
   - If using dried wakame seaweed, soak it in water for about 10-15 minutes until it expands and becomes tender. Drain and cut into bite-sized pieces.
2. **Heat the Broth:**
   - In a pot, heat the dashi broth over medium heat. Bring it to a gentle simmer.
3. **Add Flavorings:**
   - If using, add minced garlic to the simmering broth and cook for 1-2 minutes until fragrant.
   - Stir in the soy sauce and mirin, if using. Adjust the seasoning to your taste.
4. **Add Miso Paste:**
   - In a small bowl, ladle out a small amount of hot broth and whisk in the miso paste until smooth. This helps to dissolve the miso paste and prevent clumping.
   - Stir the miso mixture back into the pot. Do not let the soup boil once the miso paste has been added, as boiling can affect the flavor and texture of the miso.
5. **Add Tofu and Seaweed:**
   - Gently stir in the tofu cubes and soaked wakame seaweed. Heat the soup for an additional 2-3 minutes, until the tofu is warmed through and the seaweed is tender.
6. **Garnish and Serve:**
   - Ladle the soup into bowls.
   - Garnish with sliced green onions.
   - Serve hot.

Tips:

- **Miso:** Adjust the amount of miso paste according to your taste. White miso is milder and sweeter, while red miso has a stronger, saltier flavor.

- **Broth:** Homemade dashi provides the best flavor, but store-bought dashi or other clear broths can be used.
- **Seaweed:** Besides wakame, you can use other types of seaweed if you prefer, but wakame is most commonly used in miso soup.
- **Tofu:** Firm tofu holds its shape better in the soup, but silken tofu gives a softer texture. Use whichever you prefer.

Miso Soup with Seaweed is a delicious and nutritious dish that's quick to prepare and perfect for any time of year. The combination of miso, seaweed, and tofu makes for a flavorful and comforting bowl of soup. Enjoy!

Shrimp Tempura Udon

Ingredients:

For the Udon:

- **2 servings fresh or dried udon noodles** (if using dried, cook according to package instructions)
- **4 cups dashi broth** (or chicken/vegetable broth)
- **1/4 cup soy sauce**
- **2 tablespoons mirin** (sweet rice wine)
- **1 tablespoon sake** (Japanese rice wine, optional)
- **1 tablespoon sugar** (adjust to taste)

For the Tempura:

- **8-10 large shrimp** (peeled and deveined)
- **1 cup all-purpose flour**
- **1 cup cornstarch**
- **1 egg** (lightly beaten)
- **1 cup ice-cold water**
- **1/2 teaspoon baking powder** (optional, for extra crispiness)
- **Vegetable oil** (for frying)

For Garnish:

- **Sliced green onions**
- **Tempura dipping sauce** (Tentsuyu, optional)
- **Shredded nori (seaweed)**
- **Pickled ginger** (optional)
- **Sesame seeds** (optional)

Instructions:

1. **Prepare the Tempura:**
    - In a large bowl, combine flour, cornstarch, and baking powder (if using). Mix well.
    - In another bowl, whisk together the egg and ice-cold water. Pour this mixture into the flour mixture and stir lightly. The batter should be lumpy; do not overmix.
    - Heat vegetable oil in a deep pot or frying pan to 350°F (175°C).
    - Dip each shrimp into the batter, allowing any excess to drip off. Fry in the hot oil until golden and crispy, about 2-3 minutes. Do not overcrowd the pan.
    - Remove the shrimp with a slotted spoon and drain on paper towels.
2. **Prepare the Udon Soup:**

- In a pot, combine dashi broth, soy sauce, mirin, sake (if using), and sugar. Bring to a simmer over medium heat, stirring occasionally.
- Add the udon noodles to the pot and heat through for about 2-3 minutes, until the noodles are warmed and the flavors have melded.

3. **Assemble the Dish:**
   - Divide the cooked udon noodles between serving bowls.
   - Ladle the hot broth over the noodles.
   - Top each bowl with 4-5 pieces of shrimp tempura.
   - Garnish with sliced green onions, shredded nori, and sesame seeds. Add pickled ginger if desired.

4. **Serve:**
   - Serve immediately while hot.

Tips:

- **Batter:** Keep the batter cold and the water ice-cold to ensure crispiness. Do not overmix; lumps in the batter help create a crispy texture.
- **Oil Temperature:** Make sure the oil is at the right temperature (350°F/175°C) before frying. If the oil is too hot, the tempura will burn; if too cold, it will be greasy.
- **Noodles:** Fresh udon noodles provide the best texture, but dried noodles can also be used. Cook according to package instructions if using dried.

Shrimp Tempura Udon is a delightful combination of flavors and textures, making it a satisfying meal that's perfect for any time of year. Enjoy this comforting and delicious dish!

Tori Soboro Don

Ingredients:

For the Tori Soboro:

- **1 lb (450g) ground chicken**
- **1 tablespoon vegetable oil**
- **1 small onion** (finely chopped)
- **2 cloves garlic** (minced)
- **2 tablespoons soy sauce**
- **2 tablespoons mirin** (sweet rice wine)
- **1 tablespoon sugar** (adjust to taste)
- **1 tablespoon sake** (Japanese rice wine, optional)
- **1/4 cup water** (adjust if needed)
- **1 teaspoon sesame oil** (for added flavor, optional)

For the Rice Bowl:

- **2 cups cooked white rice** (short-grain or medium-grain)
- **2 green onions** (sliced thinly, for garnish)
- **Pickled ginger** (for garnish, optional)
- **Shredded nori (seaweed)** (for garnish, optional)
- **Sesame seeds** (for garnish, optional)

Instructions:

1. **Prepare the Tori Soboro:**
    - Heat vegetable oil in a large skillet over medium heat.
    - Add the finely chopped onion and cook until translucent, about 5 minutes.
    - Add the minced garlic and cook for an additional 1 minute until fragrant.
    - Add the ground chicken to the skillet. Cook, breaking up the meat with a spatula, until it's fully cooked and browned.
    - Stir in the soy sauce, mirin, sugar, and sake (if using). Add water if needed to reach the desired consistency. Simmer for about 5 minutes, allowing the flavors to meld and the sauce to slightly reduce.
    - If using, drizzle with sesame oil for additional flavor.
2. **Prepare the Rice Bowl:**
    - Divide the cooked rice between bowls.
    - Spoon the cooked Tori Soboro over the rice.
3. **Garnish and Serve:**
    - Garnish with sliced green onions, pickled ginger, shredded nori, and sesame seeds if desired.

- Serve hot.

Tips:

- **Ground Chicken:** You can use a mix of white and dark meat chicken for more flavor. If you prefer, ground turkey can be used as a substitute.
- **Sweetness:** Adjust the amount of sugar and mirin to suit your taste. Some prefer a sweeter flavor, while others might like it less sweet.
- **Rice:** Short-grain or medium-grain rice is typical for this dish, but other types of rice can be used as well.

Tori Soboro Don is a delicious and easy-to-make dish that provides a wonderful balance of savory and sweet flavors. It's perfect for a quick weeknight dinner or a comforting meal at any time. Enjoy!

Beef Udon

Ingredients:

For the Broth:

- **4 cups dashi broth** (or chicken/vegetable broth)
- **1/4 cup soy sauce**
- **2 tablespoons mirin** (sweet rice wine)
- **1 tablespoon sake** (Japanese rice wine, optional)
- **1 tablespoon sugar** (adjust to taste)
- **1 tablespoon miso paste** (optional, for extra depth of flavor)

For the Beef:

- **8 oz (225g) beef sirloin or ribeye** (thinly sliced)
- **1 tablespoon vegetable oil**

For the Noodles:

- **2 servings fresh or dried udon noodles** (if using dried, cook according to package instructions)

For Garnish:

- **2-3 green onions** (sliced thinly)
- **1/2 cup mushrooms** (shiitake, button, or any variety, sliced)
- **1 cup bok choy or spinach** (chopped, optional)
- **Shredded nori (seaweed)** (optional)
- **Sesame seeds** (optional)
- **Pickled ginger** (optional)

Instructions:

1. **Prepare the Broth:**
   - In a pot, combine the dashi broth, soy sauce, mirin, sake (if using), and sugar. Bring to a simmer over medium heat.
   - If using miso paste, whisk it into a small amount of hot broth to dissolve it before adding it to the pot. This step helps to avoid clumping.
   - Simmer the broth for 5 minutes, then adjust seasoning to taste.
2. **Prepare the Beef:**
   - Heat vegetable oil in a large skillet over medium-high heat.

- Add the thinly sliced beef to the skillet and cook until browned and cooked through, about 2-3 minutes per side. Remove the beef from the skillet and set aside.
3. **Cook the Noodles:**
    - If using fresh udon noodles, cook them according to the package instructions. If using dried udon noodles, follow the package directions for cooking. Drain and set aside.
4. **Combine Ingredients:**
    - In the pot with the simmering broth, add the mushrooms and cook for 3-4 minutes, until tender.
    - Add the cooked beef and bok choy or spinach to the pot. Simmer for another 1-2 minutes until the vegetables are wilted and the beef is heated through.
    - Gently stir in the cooked udon noodles, heating everything through.
5. **Serve:**
    - Divide the beef udon mixture between serving bowls.
    - Garnish with sliced green onions, shredded nori, sesame seeds, and pickled ginger if desired.
    - Serve hot.

Tips:

- **Beef:** For the best texture, slice the beef thinly against the grain. You can also use pre-sliced beef for convenience.
- **Broth:** Adjust the seasoning based on your taste preferences. You can add more soy sauce or a bit of salt if needed.
- **Noodles:** Fresh udon noodles are ideal, but dried udon noodles work well too. Be sure to cook them according to the package instructions to achieve the best texture.

Beef Udon is a warm, comforting dish with rich flavors and satisfying textures. It's perfect for a quick dinner or a special treat on a chilly day. Enjoy!

Tonkotsu Stew

Ingredients:

For the Stew:

- **2 lbs (900g) pork belly** or pork shoulder, cut into chunks
- **2 tablespoons vegetable oil**
- **1 onion** (diced)
- **2 cloves garlic** (minced)
- **1-inch piece of ginger** (grated)
- **3 carrots** (peeled and cut into chunks)
- **2 potatoes** (peeled and cut into chunks)
- **1 cup shiitake mushrooms** (sliced, or use any mushrooms you like)
- **1 cup daikon radish** (peeled and cut into chunks, optional)
- **4 cups chicken or vegetable broth**
- **1/4 cup soy sauce**
- **2 tablespoons miso paste** (white or red miso)
- **2 tablespoons sake** (Japanese rice wine, optional)
- **2 tablespoons mirin** (sweet rice wine)
- **1 tablespoon sugar** (adjust to taste)
- **1 tablespoon sesame oil** (optional, for added flavor)

For Garnish (optional):

- **Chopped green onions**
- **Sesame seeds**
- **Pickled ginger**

Instructions:

1. **Prepare the Pork:**
    - Heat vegetable oil in a large pot or Dutch oven over medium-high heat.
    - Add the pork belly or pork shoulder chunks and sear on all sides until browned. Remove the pork from the pot and set aside.
2. **Prepare the Aromatics:**
    - In the same pot, add diced onion and cook until translucent, about 5 minutes.
    - Stir in minced garlic and grated ginger, cooking for an additional 1 minute until fragrant.
3. **Build the Stew:**
    - Return the browned pork to the pot. Add carrots, potatoes, mushrooms, and daikon radish (if using).
    - Pour in the chicken or vegetable broth and bring to a boil.

- Reduce the heat to low and simmer for about 45 minutes to 1 hour, or until the pork is tender and the vegetables are cooked through.

4. **Add Flavorings:**
    - In a small bowl, whisk together soy sauce, miso paste, sake (if using), mirin, and sugar.
    - Stir this mixture into the pot with the stew. Simmer for an additional 10-15 minutes, allowing the flavors to meld and the stew to thicken slightly.

5. **Finish and Serve:**
    - If using sesame oil, stir it into the stew just before serving.
    - Taste and adjust seasoning if necessary.

6. **Garnish and Serve:**
    - Ladle the stew into bowls.
    - Garnish with chopped green onions, sesame seeds, and pickled ginger if desired.
    - Serve hot.

Tips:

- **Pork:** Pork belly adds a rich, fatty flavor to the stew, but pork shoulder is a leaner alternative. Both work well, so choose based on your preference.
- **Miso:** White miso is milder and sweeter, while red miso has a stronger flavor. Adjust based on your taste preference.
- **Thickening:** If you prefer a thicker stew, you can mash some of the vegetables or add a slurry made from cornstarch and water.

Tonkotsu Stew is a comforting and hearty dish that's perfect for a satisfying meal. Its rich flavors and tender ingredients make it a favorite for chilly days or when you're craving something comforting and filling. Enjoy!

Okonomiyaki

Ingredients:

For the Batter:

- **1 cup all-purpose flour**
- **1 cup dashi stock** (or water as a substitute)
- **1 large egg**
- **1 cup shredded cabbage** (about 1/4 head of cabbage)
- **1/4 cup finely chopped green onions** (optional)
- **1/4 cup cooked bacon, pork belly, or seafood** (optional, cut into small pieces)
- **1/2 cup tempura scraps (tenkasu)** (optional, for added crunch)

For Toppings:

- **Okonomiyaki sauce** (store-bought or homemade, see recipe below)
- **Japanese mayonnaise**
- **Bonito flakes** (katsuobushi)
- **Aonori (dried seaweed flakes)**
- **Pickled ginger** (beni shoga, optional)

Optional Fillings and Toppings:

- **Sliced mushrooms**
- **Corn kernels**
- **Shredded cheese**
- **Cooked shrimp or squid**
- **Thinly sliced pork belly or bacon**

Instructions:

1. **Prepare the Batter:**
   - In a large bowl, whisk together the flour and dashi stock until smooth.
   - Add the egg and mix until well combined.
   - Stir in the shredded cabbage, green onions, and any optional ingredients like bacon or tempura scraps. Mix until everything is well coated with the batter.
2. **Cook the Okonomiyaki:**
   - Heat a non-stick skillet or griddle over medium heat and lightly oil it.
   - Pour a portion of the batter onto the skillet, spreading it into a circle about 1/2 inch thick.
   - Cook for 3-4 minutes on one side until bubbles appear on the surface and the edges begin to look set.

- Flip the okonomiyaki and cook for another 3-4 minutes on the other side until it's cooked through and golden brown.
3. **Prepare Toppings:**
   - Once cooked, transfer the okonomiyaki to a plate.
   - Drizzle with okonomiyaki sauce and Japanese mayonnaise.
   - Sprinkle with bonito flakes, aonori, and pickled ginger if using.
4. **Serve:**
   - Serve hot, cut into slices.

Homemade Okonomiyaki Sauce:

If you want to make your own okonomiyaki sauce, here's a simple recipe:

Ingredients:

- **1/4 cup ketchup**
- **2 tablespoons Worcestershire sauce**
- **2 tablespoons soy sauce**
- **1 tablespoon mirin** (sweet rice wine)
- **1 tablespoon sugar**
- **1 teaspoon Dijon mustard**

Instructions:

1. Combine all ingredients in a bowl and mix well.
2. Adjust the seasoning to taste. Add more sugar if you like it sweeter or more Worcestershire sauce for a tangier flavor.

Tips:

- **Texture:** The batter should be thick but spreadable. Adjust the amount of dashi stock or flour as needed to get the right consistency.
- **Cooking:** Don't overcrowd the skillet. Cook in batches if necessary to ensure each okonomiyaki gets a nice, crispy exterior.
- **Toppings:** Feel free to customize the toppings and fillings to suit your taste. Okonomiyaki is highly versatile!

Okonomiyaki is a fun and delicious dish that can be tailored to your preferences, making it perfect for a casual meal or gathering. Enjoy experimenting with different ingredients and toppings!

Niku Jaga

Ingredients:

- **1 lb (450g) beef sirloin or ribeye** (sliced thinly against the grain)
- **2 tablespoons vegetable oil**
- **1 onion** (sliced thinly)
- **2 medium potatoes** (peeled and cut into bite-sized chunks)
- **1 carrot** (peeled and sliced into rounds or chunks)
- **1 cup dashi stock** (or water as a substitute)
- **1/4 cup soy sauce**
- **2 tablespoons mirin** (sweet rice wine)
- **2 tablespoons sugar** (adjust to taste)
- **1 tablespoon sake** (Japanese rice wine, optional)
- **1 tablespoon vegetable oil** (for cooking)

For Garnish (optional):

- **Chopped green onions**
- **Sesame seeds**
- **Shredded nori (seaweed)**

Instructions:

1. **Prepare the Ingredients:**
    - Slice the beef thinly. Cut the potatoes and carrots into bite-sized pieces. Slice the onion thinly.
2. **Cook the Beef:**
    - Heat vegetable oil in a large pot or Dutch oven over medium-high heat.
    - Add the sliced beef and cook until browned, about 2-3 minutes. Remove the beef from the pot and set aside.
3. **Cook the Vegetables:**
    - In the same pot, add a bit more vegetable oil if needed.
    - Add the sliced onions and cook until softened, about 5 minutes.
    - Add the potatoes and carrots, and cook for another 3-4 minutes, stirring occasionally.
4. **Simmer:**
    - Return the cooked beef to the pot with the vegetables.
    - Pour in the dashi stock (or water) and add the soy sauce, mirin, sugar, and sake (if using).
    - Bring the mixture to a boil, then reduce the heat to low. Simmer, covered, for about 20-25 minutes, or until the potatoes and carrots are tender and the sauce has thickened slightly.

5. **Finish:**
    - Taste and adjust the seasoning if needed. If the stew is too salty, add a bit of water or a touch more sugar.
    - If you prefer a thicker sauce, you can simmer uncovered for a few additional minutes to reduce the liquid.
6. **Serve:**
    - Ladle the Niku Jaga into bowls.
    - Garnish with chopped green onions, sesame seeds, or shredded nori if desired.

Tips:

- **Beef:** Thinly slice the beef against the grain to ensure tenderness. You can use beef strips or even ground beef if preferred.
- **Potatoes:** Use starchy potatoes like russets for a creamier texture. If you use waxy potatoes, they might hold their shape better but could be less creamy.
- **Sweetness:** Adjust the sugar to your taste. Some like it sweeter, while others prefer it less so.

Niku Jaga is a delicious and comforting stew that embodies the essence of Japanese home cooking. Its savory and slightly sweet flavors make it a favorite for family dinners. Enjoy!

Japanese Meatballs
Ingredients:

For the Meatballs:

- **1 lb (450g) ground chicken** (preferably a mix of dark and white meat for better flavor)
- **1/4 cup panko breadcrumbs**
- **1/4 cup finely chopped green onions**
- **1 egg** (lightly beaten)
- **2 tablespoons soy sauce**
- **1 tablespoon mirin** (sweet rice wine)
- **1 tablespoon sake** (Japanese rice wine, optional)
- **1 tablespoon ginger** (grated)
- **2 cloves garlic** (minced)
- **1 teaspoon sesame oil**
- **Salt and pepper** (to taste)

For the Glaze (optional):

- **1/4 cup soy sauce**
- **2 tablespoons mirin**
- **2 tablespoons sugar**
- **1 tablespoon sake** (optional)

For Garnish:

- **Chopped green onions**
- **Sesame seeds**

Instructions:

1. **Prepare the Meatball Mixture:**
   - In a large bowl, combine the ground chicken, panko breadcrumbs, chopped green onions, beaten egg, soy sauce, mirin, sake (if using), grated ginger, minced garlic, sesame oil, salt, and pepper.
   - Mix until well combined but don't overmix, as this can make the meatballs dense.
2. **Form the Meatballs:**
   - Wet your hands slightly to prevent sticking, then shape the mixture into 1- to 1.5-inch meatballs. You should get about 12-15 meatballs, depending on size.
3. **Cook the Meatballs:**
   - **Pan-Frying Method:**
     - Heat a non-stick skillet or frying pan over medium heat and add a small amount of oil.

- Add the meatballs and cook, turning occasionally, until they are browned on all sides and cooked through, about 8-10 minutes.
  - **Grilling Method:**
    - Preheat your grill or grill pan to medium-high heat.
    - Thread the meatballs onto skewers if using a grill, or place them directly on the grill.
    - Grill, turning occasionally, until they are nicely charred and cooked through, about 8-10 minutes.
4. **Prepare the Glaze (optional):**
   - In a small saucepan, combine soy sauce, mirin, sugar, and sake (if using).
   - Bring to a simmer over medium heat, stirring until the sugar has dissolved and the sauce has slightly thickened, about 5 minutes.
5. **Serve:**
   - Brush the cooked meatballs with the glaze if using, or serve with a dipping sauce on the side.
   - Garnish with chopped green onions and sesame seeds if desired.

Tips:

- **Texture:** For tender meatballs, be careful not to overmix the meat mixture.
- **Flavor:** You can also add other ingredients to the meatball mixture, such as finely chopped mushrooms or a bit of chili flakes for extra flavor.
- **Glaze:** The glaze adds a nice shine and extra flavor to the meatballs, but they are also delicious on their own.

Japanese Meatballs are versatile and can be enjoyed in many ways—served on skewers, in a bowl with rice, or as an appetizer. Enjoy making and eating these flavorful, juicy meatballs!

Pork and Vegetable Hot Pot

Ingredients:

For the Broth:

- **4 cups dashi stock** (or chicken/vegetable broth)
- **1/4 cup soy sauce**
- **2 tablespoons mirin** (sweet rice wine)
- **1 tablespoon sake** (Japanese rice wine, optional)
- **1 tablespoon sugar** (adjust to taste)

For the Hot Pot:

- **1 lb (450g) pork shoulder or pork belly** (sliced thinly, about 1/8 inch thick)
- **1 cup shiitake mushrooms** (sliced, or use any mushrooms you like)
- **2 cups napa cabbage** (cut into bite-sized pieces)
- **2 medium carrots** (peeled and sliced thinly)
- **1 cup daikon radish** (peeled and sliced thinly, optional)
- **1 cup enoki mushrooms** (optional)
- **1 cup spinach or bok choy** (optional)
- **1 onion** (sliced thinly)
- **Tofu** (firm or silken, cut into cubes, optional)
- **1-2 green onions** (sliced, for garnish)
- **Sesame seeds** (for garnish, optional)

For Dipping Sauce (optional):

- **1/4 cup soy sauce**
- **1 tablespoon rice vinegar**
- **1 tablespoon sesame oil**
- **1 teaspoon sugar**
- **1 clove garlic** (minced)
- **1 teaspoon grated ginger**

Instructions:

1. **Prepare the Broth:**
   - In a large pot or hot pot, combine the dashi stock, soy sauce, mirin, sake (if using), and sugar.
   - Bring to a simmer over medium heat, stirring until the sugar is dissolved. Keep warm on low heat.
2. **Prepare the Ingredients:**

- Slice the pork thinly and prepare all vegetables and tofu.
- Arrange the vegetables and tofu on a large platter for easy access during cooking.

3. **Cook the Hot Pot:**
     - Add a few slices of pork to the simmering broth and cook until they are no longer pink, about 1-2 minutes.
     - Add the vegetables, tofu, and mushrooms to the pot. Cook until the vegetables are tender and the tofu is heated through, about 5-10 minutes.
4. **Serve:**
     - Transfer the hot pot to a serving table or dining area with a portable burner to keep it warm.
     - Serve the hot pot directly from the pot. Use chopsticks or ladles to serve portions of meat, vegetables, and broth into individual bowls.
5. **Prepare the Dipping Sauce (optional):**
     - In a small bowl, mix together soy sauce, rice vinegar, sesame oil, sugar, minced garlic, and grated ginger.
     - Serve as a dipping sauce for the meat and vegetables.

Tips:

- **Broth:** You can adjust the seasoning of the broth to your taste. Add more soy sauce for saltiness or more sugar for sweetness.
- **Vegetables:** Feel free to use any vegetables you like or have on hand. Common additions include mushrooms, bell peppers, and cabbage.
- **Tofu:** Use firm tofu if you prefer it to hold its shape better during cooking. Silken tofu will be softer and may break apart more easily.
- **Serving:** The hot pot is best enjoyed hot and fresh. Keep the broth simmering throughout the meal to maintain the temperature.

Pork and Vegetable Hot Pot is a delicious, warming dish that brings people together around the table. It's perfect for a cozy family dinner or gathering with friends. Enjoy!

Kinpira Gobo

Ingredients:

- **1 large burdock root** (gobo, about 8-10 inches long)
- **1 large carrot**
- **1 tablespoon vegetable oil**
- **2 tablespoons soy sauce**
- **2 tablespoons mirin** (sweet rice wine)
- **1 tablespoon sugar** (adjust to taste)
- **1 tablespoon sake** (optional, Japanese rice wine)
- **1 tablespoon sesame seeds** (toasted, optional for garnish)
- **1 teaspoon sesame oil** (optional, for added flavor)
- **Red chili pepper flakes** (optional, for heat)
- **1-2 green onions** (chopped, optional for garnish)

Instructions:

1. **Prepare the Burdock Root:**
    - Scrub the burdock root under running water to remove any dirt. Peel the root with a vegetable peeler or knife if desired.
    - Slice the burdock root into thin julienne strips. To prevent discoloration, soak the slices in a bowl of water with a splash of vinegar or lemon juice while you prepare the other ingredients.
2. **Prepare the Carrot:**
    - Peel the carrot and slice it into thin julienne strips, similar in size to the burdock root.
3. **Cook the Vegetables:**
    - Heat vegetable oil in a large skillet or wok over medium heat.
    - Add the burdock root and carrot strips. Stir-fry for about 5-7 minutes until they begin to soften and become fragrant.
4. **Add Seasonings:**
    - Add the soy sauce, mirin, sugar, and sake (if using) to the skillet. Stir well to coat the vegetables evenly with the sauce.
    - Continue to cook for another 5-7 minutes, stirring occasionally, until the vegetables are tender and the liquid has reduced to a syrupy consistency.
5. **Finish and Serve:**
    - If using, drizzle with sesame oil for additional flavor.
    - Sprinkle with toasted sesame seeds and red chili pepper flakes if desired.
    - Garnish with chopped green onions if you like.
6. **Serve:**
    - Serve warm or at room temperature as a side dish.

Tips:

- **Burdock Root:** Fresh burdock root can be found at Asian grocery stores. If you can't find it, you can substitute with thinly sliced celery or other crunchy vegetables, though the flavor and texture will be different.
- **Carrots:** Julienne the carrots to match the size of the burdock root for even cooking.
- **Sweetness and Saltiness:** Adjust the sugar and soy sauce to your taste. Some variations are sweeter or saltier depending on preference.
- **Toasting Sesame Seeds:** Toast sesame seeds in a dry pan over medium heat until golden brown for added flavor.

Kinpira Gobo is a nutritious and flavorful dish with a delightful balance of sweet and savory elements. It's a great way to enjoy the unique taste of burdock root and adds a delicious crunch to any meal. Enjoy!

Sweet and Sour Pork

Ingredients:

For the Pork:

- **1 lb (450g) pork shoulder or pork loin** (cut into bite-sized chunks)
- **1/2 cup all-purpose flour**
- **1/4 cup cornstarch**
- **1 large egg** (beaten)
- **1 cup vegetable oil** (for frying)
- **Salt and pepper** (to taste)

For the Sweet and Sour Sauce:

- **1/2 cup ketchup**
- **1/4 cup rice vinegar** (or white vinegar)
- **1/4 cup sugar** (adjust to taste)
- **2 tablespoons soy sauce**
- **1 tablespoon soy sauce** (for additional depth of flavor, optional)
- **1 tablespoon cornstarch** (mixed with 2 tablespoons water to make a slurry)
- **1/2 cup pineapple juice** (from a can of pineapple, or store-bought)
- **1 clove garlic** (minced)
- **1 teaspoon grated ginger**
- **1/4 teaspoon red pepper flakes** (optional, for a bit of heat)

For the Vegetables (optional):

- **1 bell pepper** (cut into chunks, any color)
- **1 onion** (cut into chunks)
- **1 cup pineapple chunks** (canned or fresh)
- **1 cup snap peas or carrots** (sliced)

For Garnish:

- **Chopped green onions**
- **Sesame seeds**

Instructions:

1. **Prepare the Pork:**
    - Season the pork chunks with salt and pepper.

- In a bowl, mix together flour and cornstarch. Dredge the pork chunks in the flour mixture, then dip them in the beaten egg, and dredge again in the flour mixture to coat evenly.
2. **Fry the Pork:**
   - Heat vegetable oil in a large skillet or wok over medium-high heat.
   - Fry the coated pork chunks in batches, being careful not to overcrowd the pan. Cook until they are golden brown and crispy, about 4-5 minutes per batch.
   - Remove the pork from the oil and drain on paper towels. Set aside.
3. **Prepare the Sauce:**
   - In a saucepan, combine ketchup, rice vinegar, sugar, soy sauce, additional soy sauce (if using), and pineapple juice. Stir well.
   - Add minced garlic, grated ginger, and red pepper flakes (if using).
   - Bring the mixture to a simmer over medium heat, stirring occasionally.
   - Once the sauce starts to bubble, add the cornstarch slurry and continue to simmer until the sauce thickens, about 2-3 minutes.
4. **Add Vegetables (Optional):**
   - If using vegetables, heat a little oil in a separate pan or add to the same pan used for frying.
   - Stir-fry the bell peppers, onions, snap peas, and carrots until they are slightly tender but still crisp, about 3-4 minutes.
   - Add the pineapple chunks and cook for an additional minute.
5. **Combine:**
   - Add the fried pork chunks to the sauce and toss to coat evenly.
   - If you've prepared vegetables, add them to the pan with the pork and sauce, and stir to combine everything well.
6. **Serve:**
   - Garnish with chopped green onions and sesame seeds.
   - Serve hot over steamed rice.

Tips:

- **Pork:** For the crispiest results, make sure the oil is hot enough before frying. You can test the oil temperature by dropping a small piece of batter into the oil; it should sizzle immediately.
- **Sauce:** Adjust the sweetness and tanginess of the sauce according to your taste. More sugar will increase sweetness, while more vinegar will add tang.
- **Vegetables:** Adding vegetables not only enhances the flavor but also adds color and nutrition to the dish.

Sweet and Sour Pork is a delightful dish that combines crispy pork with a tangy, sweet sauce, making it a favorite for many. Enjoy preparing and savoring this classic dish!

Japanese Mushroom Soup

Ingredients:

- **200g (7 oz) mixed mushrooms** (shiitake, enoki, maitake, or any other variety you like)
- **4 cups dashi stock** (or vegetable/chicken broth as a substitute)
- **1 tablespoon soy sauce**
- **1 tablespoon mirin** (sweet rice wine)
- **1 teaspoon sake** (optional, Japanese rice wine)
- **1/2 block tofu** (cubed, firm or silken tofu)
- **1-2 green onions** (sliced thinly)
- **1 sheet nori** (seaweed, cut into strips or shredded, optional)
- **1 tablespoon miso paste** (optional, for added depth of flavor)
- **1 teaspoon sesame oil** (optional, for added flavor)
- **1 clove garlic** (minced, optional for extra flavor)
- **1 teaspoon grated ginger** (optional for extra flavor)
- **Salt and pepper** (to taste)

Instructions:

1. **Prepare the Mushrooms:**
   - Clean and slice the mushrooms. If using enoki mushrooms, trim the ends and separate them into smaller clusters.
   - If you're using dried mushrooms, rehydrate them in warm water for about 20 minutes, then slice.
2. **Prepare the Broth:**
   - In a large pot, bring the dashi stock (or broth) to a simmer over medium heat.
   - Add the soy sauce, mirin, and sake (if using). Stir well.
3. **Cook the Mushrooms:**
   - Add the sliced mushrooms to the pot. Simmer for about 5-7 minutes, or until the mushrooms are tender.
4. **Add Tofu and Optional Ingredients:**
   - Gently add the cubed tofu to the pot. If using miso paste, dissolve it in a small amount of hot broth before adding it to the soup to ensure it mixes well. Stir to combine.
   - If adding garlic and ginger, you can sauté them in a separate pan with sesame oil and then add them to the soup for an extra layer of flavor.
5. **Season and Garnish:**
   - Taste the soup and adjust seasoning with salt and pepper if needed.
   - Garnish with sliced green onions, nori strips, or shredded seaweed if desired.
6. **Serve:**
   - Ladle the soup into bowls and serve hot.

Tips:

- **Mushrooms:** Use a mix of fresh mushrooms for the best flavor. Shiitake and enoki are commonly used, but feel free to experiment with other varieties.
- **Dashi Stock:** For a more authentic flavor, use dashi stock. If you prefer a vegetarian version, you can use kombu (seaweed) dashi or vegetable broth.
- **Miso:** Adding miso paste provides extra umami and richness to the soup, but it's optional depending on your preference.

Japanese Mushroom Soup is a light yet flavorful soup that's easy to make and perfect for a comforting meal. Enjoy this umami-packed dish!

Tofu and Pork Hot Pot

Ingredients:

For the Broth:

- **4 cups dashi stock** (or chicken/vegetable broth)
- **1/4 cup soy sauce**
- **2 tablespoons mirin** (sweet rice wine)
- **1 tablespoon sake** (Japanese rice wine, optional)
- **1 tablespoon sugar** (adjust to taste)

For the Hot Pot:

- **1 lb (450g) pork shoulder or pork belly** (sliced thinly against the grain)
- **1 block firm tofu** (cut into cubes)
- **2 cups napa cabbage** (cut into bite-sized pieces)
- **1 cup shiitake mushrooms** (sliced, or use any mushrooms you like)
- **1 cup sliced carrots** (optional)
- **1 cup enoki mushrooms** (optional)
- **1-2 green onions** (sliced)
- **1 small daikon radish** (peeled and sliced thinly, optional)
- **1 tablespoon vegetable oil** (for cooking)

For Garnish (optional):

- **Chopped green onions**
- **Sesame seeds**
- **Fresh cilantro** (optional)

Instructions:

1. **Prepare the Broth:**
    - In a large pot or hot pot, combine the dashi stock, soy sauce, mirin, sake (if using), and sugar.
    - Bring to a simmer over medium heat, stirring until the sugar is dissolved. Keep warm on low heat.
2. **Prepare the Ingredients:**
    - Slice the pork thinly against the grain.
    - Cut the tofu into bite-sized cubes.
    - Prepare and slice the vegetables and mushrooms.
3. **Cook the Hot Pot:**
    - Heat vegetable oil in a large skillet or hot pot over medium-high heat.

- Add the sliced pork and cook until it is just browned but not fully cooked through, about 2-3 minutes.
- Transfer the pork to the pot with the broth.

4. **Simmer:**
    - Add the tofu and vegetables (cabbage, mushrooms, carrots, daikon) to the pot.
    - Simmer gently until the vegetables are tender and the pork is fully cooked, about 10-15 minutes. Stir occasionally.

5. **Serve:**
    - Garnish with sliced green onions, sesame seeds, and fresh cilantro if desired.
    - Serve hot, ladling the hot pot into bowls with some of the broth and ingredients.

Tips:

- **Pork:** Use thinly sliced pork for quicker cooking. Pork belly adds a rich flavor, but pork shoulder is a leaner option.
- **Tofu:** Firm tofu works best as it holds its shape during cooking. Silken tofu may break apart more easily.
- **Vegetables:** Feel free to add other vegetables like mushrooms, bok choy, or snow peas based on your preference.
- **Serving:** Keep the hot pot warm throughout the meal using a portable burner or hot plate.

Tofu and Pork Hot Pot is a versatile and comforting dish that combines the richness of pork with the delicate texture of tofu and the flavors of a savory broth. Enjoy this warming meal with family and friends!

Spicy Miso Ramen

Ingredients:

For the Broth:

- **4 cups chicken or vegetable broth**
- **2 tablespoons miso paste** (red or white miso, or a combination)
- **2 tablespoons soy sauce**
- **1 tablespoon sesame oil**
- **1 tablespoon chili paste** (such as doubanjiang or sambal oelek, adjust to taste)
- **1 tablespoon grated ginger**
- **2 cloves garlic** (minced)
- **1 tablespoon rice vinegar** (optional, for a touch of acidity)
- **1 teaspoon sugar** (optional, for a touch of sweetness)

For the Toppings:

- **2 servings ramen noodles** (fresh or dried)
- **1 cup bean sprouts** (blanched or sautéed)
- **1 cup spinach** (blanched or sautéed)
- **1 cup sliced mushrooms** (shiitake, cremini, or enoki, sautéed if desired)
- **2 green onions** (sliced)
- **1-2 boiled eggs** (soft-boiled or marinated)
- **1/2 cup corn kernels** (optional, for added sweetness)
- **1 sheet nori** (seaweed, cut into strips)
- **Sesame seeds** (for garnish)
- **Fresh cilantro** (optional, for garnish)
- **Chili oil** (optional, for extra heat)

Instructions:

1. **Prepare the Broth:**
   - Heat sesame oil in a large pot over medium heat.
   - Add minced garlic and grated ginger. Sauté until fragrant, about 1-2 minutes.
   - Add chili paste and cook for another minute to release its flavors.
   - Pour in the chicken or vegetable broth and bring to a simmer.
   - Stir in the miso paste until completely dissolved.
   - Add soy sauce, rice vinegar (if using), and sugar (if using). Adjust seasoning to taste.
   - Simmer the broth for about 10 minutes to allow the flavors to meld.
2. **Cook the Noodles:**
   - Cook the ramen noodles according to package instructions. Drain and set aside.

3. **Prepare the Toppings:**
   - If using boiled eggs, cook them according to your preference. Soft-boiled eggs should be cooked for about 6-7 minutes, then cooled in ice water before peeling.
   - Blanch or sauté the bean sprouts and spinach. If using mushrooms, sauté them until tender.
   - Prepare any additional toppings like corn kernels or sliced green onions.
4. **Assemble the Ramen:**
   - Divide the cooked ramen noodles between bowls.
   - Ladle the hot broth over the noodles.
   - Arrange the toppings on top of the noodles: bean sprouts, spinach, mushrooms, green onions, and corn.
   - Halve the boiled eggs and place them on top of the ramen.
   - Garnish with nori strips, sesame seeds, and fresh cilantro if desired.
   - Drizzle with chili oil for extra heat if you like.
5. **Serve:**
   - Serve the ramen hot and enjoy immediately.

Tips:

- **Miso Paste:** Red miso is more robust and salty, while white miso is milder and sweeter. You can use either or a mix depending on your taste preference.
- **Spiciness:** Adjust the amount of chili paste or oil according to your heat tolerance.
- **Noodles:** Fresh ramen noodles tend to have a better texture, but dried noodles are a convenient alternative.
- **Toppings:** Feel free to customize with additional toppings like bamboo shoots, sliced pork, or tofu.

Spicy Miso Ramen is a warming and satisfying dish that balances spicy, savory, and umami flavors. Enjoy crafting this comforting bowl of ramen!

Teriyaki Beef Bowl

Ingredients:

For the Teriyaki Sauce:

- **1/4 cup soy sauce**
- **1/4 cup mirin** (sweet rice wine)
- **1/4 cup sake** (optional, Japanese rice wine)
- **2 tablespoons brown sugar** (or honey)
- **1 tablespoon cornstarch** (mixed with 1 tablespoon water to make a slurry)
- **1 tablespoon grated ginger**
- **1 clove garlic** (minced)
- **1 teaspoon sesame oil** (optional, for flavor)

For the Beef Bowl:

- **1 lb (450g) beef sirloin or flank steak** (thinly sliced against the grain)
- **2 tablespoons vegetable oil**
- **2 cups cooked white rice** (or brown rice, for serving)
- **1 cup steamed or sautéed vegetables** (such as broccoli, bell peppers, carrots, or snap peas)
- **1 tablespoon sesame seeds** (for garnish, optional)
- **2-3 green onions** (sliced, for garnish)
- **Pickled ginger** (optional, for garnish)
- **Sliced red chili** (optional, for heat)

Instructions:

1. **Prepare the Teriyaki Sauce:**
    - In a small saucepan, combine soy sauce, mirin, sake (if using), brown sugar, grated ginger, and minced garlic.
    - Bring to a simmer over medium heat, stirring occasionally.
    - Once the sugar has dissolved, add the cornstarch slurry to the sauce while stirring continuously.
    - Continue to simmer for another 2-3 minutes until the sauce thickens.
    - Remove from heat and stir in sesame oil if using. Set aside.
2. **Cook the Beef:**
    - Heat vegetable oil in a large skillet or wok over medium-high heat.
    - Add the sliced beef to the skillet in a single layer. Cook for 2-3 minutes on each side, or until the beef is browned and cooked through. Avoid overcrowding the pan; cook in batches if necessary.

- Once the beef is cooked, pour the teriyaki sauce over the beef and toss to coat evenly. Cook for an additional 1-2 minutes until the sauce is heated through and slightly caramelized.
3. **Assemble the Bowl:**
    - Divide the cooked rice between serving bowls.
    - Top the rice with the teriyaki beef and sauce.
    - Arrange the steamed or sautéed vegetables around the beef.
    - Garnish with sesame seeds, sliced green onions, and pickled ginger if desired.
    - Add sliced red chili for extra heat if you like.
4. **Serve:**
    - Serve the Teriyaki Beef Bowl hot and enjoy immediately.

Tips:

- **Beef:** Thinly slicing the beef against the grain ensures tenderness. You can also use pre-sliced beef meant for stir-frying.
- **Rice:** For extra flavor, consider using sushi rice or jasmine rice. Brown rice can be used for a healthier option.
- **Vegetables:** Customize with your favorite vegetables or what you have on hand. Quick-steaming or sautéing will keep them vibrant and crunchy.
- **Sauce:** Adjust the sweetness and saltiness of the sauce according to your preference. You can add more sugar or soy sauce if needed.

Teriyaki Beef Bowl is a flavorful and satisfying meal that brings together tender beef and savory sauce over a bed of rice. It's perfect for a quick and delicious dinner!

Japanese Clam Soup

Ingredients:

- **1 lb (450g) fresh clams** (such as littleneck or manila clams)
- **4 cups dashi stock** (or chicken/vegetable broth as a substitute)
- **1 tablespoon soy sauce**
- **1 tablespoon mirin** (sweet rice wine)
- **1-2 teaspoons sake** (optional, Japanese rice wine)
- **1/2 teaspoon salt** (adjust to taste)
- **2 green onions** (sliced thinly)
- **1 small piece of kombu** (dried seaweed, about 4-inch square, optional for added umami)
- **1 teaspoon grated ginger** (optional)
- **1 tablespoon miso paste** (optional, for a deeper flavor)
- **Shredded nori** (seaweed, for garnish, optional)

Instructions:

1. **Prepare the Clams:**
    - Scrub the clams under cold running water to remove any sand or dirt. Soak them in a bowl of salted water for about 20-30 minutes to help them expel any sand. Drain and rinse again.
2. **Prepare the Dashi Stock (if using):**
    - If using kombu, add it to a pot with 4 cups of water and let it soak for about 30 minutes.
    - Heat the pot over medium heat until just before it starts to boil. Remove the kombu.
    - If you prefer using pre-made dashi, you can skip this step.
3. **Cook the Soup:**
    - In a large pot, bring the dashi stock to a simmer over medium heat.
    - If using sake, soy sauce, and mirin, add them to the pot along with salt. Stir to combine.
    - Add the clams to the pot and cover. Cook until the clams open, about 5-7 minutes. Discard any clams that do not open.
4. **Add Optional Ingredients:**
    - If using miso paste, dissolve it in a small amount of hot broth and add it to the pot. Stir well to combine.
    - Add grated ginger if using, and let the soup simmer for an additional 1-2 minutes.
5. **Garnish and Serve:**
    - Ladle the soup into bowls.
    - Garnish with sliced green onions and shredded nori if desired.

- Serve hot and enjoy immediately.

Tips:

- **Clams:** Ensure clams are fresh and well-cleaned. Discard any clams with cracked shells or that do not open after cooking.
- **Dashi:** If you don't have dashi, a light chicken or vegetable broth can be used, but dashi gives the soup a more authentic umami flavor.
- **Miso:** Miso adds a richer flavor but can be omitted for a lighter soup. If using miso, avoid boiling the soup after adding it to preserve its flavor and nutrients.
- **Seaweed:** Shredded nori adds a nice touch of umami and visual appeal but is optional.

Japanese Clam Soup is a simple yet elegant dish that showcases the delicate flavor of clams. It's perfect for a light meal or as an appetizer in a larger Japanese meal. Enjoy!

www.ingramcontent.com/pod-product-compliance
Lightning Source LLC
LaVergne TN
LVHW061940070526
838199LV00060B/3897